Variation
and
Linguistic Theory

CHARLES-JAMES N. BAILEY

CENTER FOR APPLIED LINGUISTICS : 1973

International Standard Book Number: 87281-032-1
Library of Congress Catalog Card Number: 73-84648

Printed in the United States of America

Students and External Readers	Staff & Research Students
DATE DUE FOR RETURN	**DATE OF ISSUE**
28.JUN 78 016	13 SEP 76 0 0 0 5
11.MAR 81 0 0	11 JAN 78 0 0 0 0 0 0
27.JUN 83 0 0 33	29 NOV 83 0 0 7 0 0
27.JUN 84 0 0 0	FOUR WEEKS ONLY -2 DEC 1992
08. FEB 96	FOUR WEEKS ONLY 4 JAN 1993
26. JUN 96	N.B. All books must be returned for the Annual Inspection in June

Any book which you borrow remains your responsibility
until the loan slip is cancelled

Dedicated to

HANSLI

and the Menehune gardens of

Moani Lehua

PREFACE

This monograph was originally put together as the basis for talks given at the 1971 Linguistic Society of America Summer Institute at the State University of New York, Buffalo. Many revisions and additions have altered the form in which it was first circulated among colleagues. It may avert misunderstanding if I here distinguish the role of the historian of ideas from that of the advocate of ideas. Both ought to credit the sources of ideas which have been advocated in such a manner as to have been influential. The historian has two additional tasks which do not seem to me to belong to the job of the advocate of ideas. He needs to record items that went unnoticed and lacked influence, especially if later they should have turned out to have been significant for the present. And the historian also needs to ascertain what a scholar (such as Saussure) really intended to convey. The advocate of ideas, on the other hand, may limit his attention to the effects which in actual fact eventuated out of a man's teachings, whether through infelicitous changes of mind or through distortions caused by his editors. This present study definitely belongs to the advocate of ideas category and not to the historical one. It is the writer's hope, not that the principles and other proposals included in this writing will necessarily prove correct; rather that they will show the feasibility of dynamic grammars and stir up discussions which -- whether they prove these proposals right or wrong -- will advance our discipline on the road toward a more realistic and adequate linguistic theory.

In preparing this volume, the writer has had the aid of both colleagues and students. The interest and help of William Labov is gratefully acknowledged, although nothing in the following pages should necessarily be assumed to be in agreement with his present views, given the differences in emphasis between us. A general acknowledgement here, and the references in the text itself, will have to suffice for those other colleagues and students who have made me aware of errors and weaknesses in my positions. A detailed listing, if at all possible, would be too long and too prone to invidious, if accidental, omissions. But the writer's students have been a constant help in exposing flaws in his attempts to arrive at working models for formulating polylectal grammar, and have also helped in providing illustrative analyses for the following pages.

Thanks are due Allene Guss Grognet who edited this volume and Freda Ahearn who typed the manuscript for publication. Finally, grateful acknowledgement is made to the National Science Foundation for funds given to the School of Languages and Linguistics, Georgetown University, for its Sociolinguistics Program, which in turn made time for revising this work possible.

C.-J.N.B.

Washington, D.C.

June 1973

CONTENTS

1 PROBLEMS WITH OLD ASSUMPTIONS

1.0 <u>Introduction</u>. During the past few years, linguists working in different branches of the discipline have increasingly shown discontent with the
framework of axioms for descriptive work which have
been widely accepted for almost half a century. Their
frustrations have led to attempts to escape from the
procrustean framework of idealized oppositions by de-
vising models that handle variation and continuums in
linguistic data, whether semantic or phonological.
While it would carry the present writing far beyond
its necessary limits to fully document such developments,[1] a proper perspective for following the remainder
of this book does seem to require mentioning in summary
fashion the main lines of these developments. First in
time has been the work of those variationists or lec-
tologists, mostly with backgrounds in historical linguistics or creole studies, whose work so far has mostly
concentrated on the social variation of language in
speech communities. Then there are the massive researches of the generative semanticists, whose investigations have led them to an awareness of the role of
<u>communicative competence</u> in the use of language and to
a new understanding of fuzziness in semantic continuums
which goes well beyond previous assumptions. At least
two schools of natural phonology, as well as the generative semanticists, have been increasingly taking notice
of implicational patterns, already familiar in recent
years to variationists.

Clear convergences among these groups, whose members have often overlapped, has been taking place on
several fronts. The theoretical importance of fine
(low-level) variation in empirical data is rapidly being acknowledged by the parties just mentioned. Continuums are replacing discrete breaks in implicational
series or squishes, fuzziness in logic, etc. The role

of force (intention or attitude) and presupposition
is now apparent in both phonology and syntax. Dis-
course analysis is replacing sentence analysis. The
use of language in its social contexts is now recognized to have important effects on the grammar. This
is beginning to change old beliefs about idiolects
and dialects. The role of time in 'synchronic' language patterning is gaining some recognition, although
this has hardly begun, or at least not gone very far,
in various quarters. These developments are having
far-reaching effects on historical linguistics (cf.
Bailey 1973a) and on transcriptional phonetics
(cf. Bailey MS). And even those who espouse the
assumptions of the old framework have begun to question
previously accepted views (e.g. those concerning rule
ordering and prosodic analysis) and are taking increasing interest in formerly disdained topics (e.g. syllable-sensitive phonological markings).
      The contribution to the new developments embodied
in the present treatment of variation in English phonology will consist of a discussion of the problems
inherent in widely held Saussurian doctrines and the
developing and illustrating of dynamic models for describing the patterning of variation within a framework
that is not purely synchronic, but which includes a
temporal dimension.[2]

1.1 The homogeneity paradox. At the beginning of the
second decade of this century, Ferdinand de Saussure
(1962:30 = 1959:14) proposed a distinction that was
destined to have ominous consequences.

      In separating langue from parole, we
      simultaneously separate: (1) what is social
      from what is individual; (2) what is essen-
      tial from what is accessory and more or
      less accidental.

Saussure often spoke of parole as equivalent to individual exécution, or production. For him, the object
of linguistic study was langue, which he likened to the
score of a symphony, not parole, which he likened to
the performance of that symphony by an orchestra--with
all its unintended mistakes. It is clear that the distinction between langue and parole entails a concentration on the essential and a disregard for what is

conceived to be accidental.[3] While linguists could
hardly demur to such sentiments,[4] there are serious
disagreements among them over where the line is to be
drawn between langue and parole, or rather between
what is viewed as essential and what is viewed as
accidental.

Saussure (1962:37 = 1959:18) himself was clear
that the study of parole belongs to "an ensemble of
disciplines whose place in linguistics is due only to
their relation to langue":

> The study of language therefore com-
> prises two divisions: the essential one has
> as its object langue, which is social in its
> essence and independent of the individual;
> this study is purely psychological; the other,
> secondary [study] has as its object the indi-
> vidual aspect of language, that is, parole,
> including phonation; it is psychophysical.

He goes on to add that his definition of langue "supposes our setting aside all that is foreign to its
organism, its system, in a word, everything that is
referred to by the term 'external linguistics'"
(1962:40 = 1949:20). He allows that external linguistics includes many important things, especially linguistic matters that have to do with ethnology. He
also mentions issues that today might be referred to
under the heading of the sociology of language. And
then he lists everything that has to do with "the
geographical extension of languages and dialectal
splitting" (1962:41 = 1959:21); in short, what has
traditionally been called dialectology. While con-
ceding the merits of the study of "external linguistic
phenomena" (1962:42 = 1959:22), Saussure firmly denies
the validity of the view that the internal linguistic
organism cannot be known without studying such external
phenomena.

It is easy to discern the contradiction between
this point of view and Saussure's social view of langue
quoted earlier. His acceptance of the view that linguistics should pursue the study of transpersonal phenomena (those which are "independent of the individual")
does not harmonize with his refusal (see §1.2) to grant
the legitimacy of studying transpersonal patterns in
which a time factor intervenes, e.g. the varieties of a

language spoken by father and grandson in the same
household. As will be seen in the next section,
Saussure makes a radical distinction between the
diachronic and the synchronic. His four-way splitting up of descriptive, historical, dialectological,
and ethnographic linguistics has been accepted with
few demurrers (most notably by Roman Jakobson). This
has resulted in a degree of theoretical isolation
among the workers in each sub-discipline from the ad-
vances in the others. The fission of linguistics into
so many different methods and theoretical outlooks for
the respective pursuits has been deleterious to the
entire discipline and has been acutely felt by the few
linguists who have pursued investigations in several
of the sub-disciplines. This has been exacerbated by
specializations within a given sub-discipline, e.g.
phonology or syntax.

   One who took seriously Saussure's social characterization of langue, or at least of language, was
Edward Sapir. After comments full of insight on the
differences between individual and communal variation
in English (1921:157), he went on to speak (158) of
"something like an ideal linguistic entity dominating
the speech habits of the members of each group". But
such a sentiment, more or less isolated in America,
was not destined to have the influence that Leonard
Bloomfield's point of view was to wield. Despite a
cautious attitude toward the variation which he recognized to be omnipresent even in individuals' speech,
Bloomfield's understanding of science induced him
'provisionally' to abstract from the 'inessential differences' between the speech of Midwesterners and
Englishmen or Southerners (1933:45). This being so,
why then did he not attempt a descriptive formulation
of English as a whole, rather than simply of one kind
of Chicago English? The answer to this question leads
us to a slightly broader survey of the development of
contemporary linguistic theory.

   For the past half century, the linguists that have
had the most influence on the discipline have regarded
it as feasible and worthwhile to limit their attention
to invariant samples of language. Although the limitations of linguistic theory in their day can account for
some of this attitude, there have been those who, so
far from fearing that this procedure would vitiate their

work, have insisted that it will lead to an adequate
theory of human language. At issue is the extent to
which a linguistic description should abstract from
variation in a language beyond the level of systematic
phonetics, a level of abstraction excluding the random
deviations which may be called performance variations.

It is something of a paradox that the greatest
degree of abstracting away from data variation has been
advocated by the empiricists. Linguistic thought in
the thirties and forties in the United States was dominated by a positivist philosophy of science and be-
haviorist methodology. The empiricist-positivist orientation (derived from mediæval nominalism through
Romanticism) stressed the reality of the individual
datum and was loath to admit the reality of abstract
relations among data. This outlook generally brings
in its train cautions against reifying 'natures'.
Bloomfield's way of having his orientational cake and
eating it too was to attend to a particular set of
homogeneous data as a means of abstracting away from
the variation that he admitted to be inherent in all
linguistic data.[5]

His thought was developed by his followers in such
a way as to insist on abstracting not only from interpersonal differences, but even from the stylistic differences of a single speaker-hearer. Abstracting from
variation (and I omit discussion of the fallacy discussed by Postal (1968:12-18)) was carried to such
lengths by Bloomfield's followers that no patterned
variation was taken to be relevant to grammars except
the distribution in mutually exclusive (complementary)
surficial environments of phones and morphs in a single
style of a given speaker. The classic example of this
doctrine is the following passage from Bernard Bloch
(1948:7-8):

> Definition. The totality of the possible
> utterances of one speaker at one time in using
> a language to interact with one other speaker
> is an idiolect... As for the words 'at one
> time',...they are included in the definition
> only because we must provide for the fact that
> a speaker's manner of speaking changes during
> his lifetime. The phrase 'with one other
> speaker' is intended to exclude the possibility

that an idiolect might embrace more than
one style of speaking....
      Definition. The process of dis-
covering [sic] different auditory fractions
of an idiolect and their different arrange-
ments is phonological analysis.
      Definition. A class of idiolects with
the same phonological system is a dialect.

Recent researches, however, have undermined the
utility of the concept of an idiolect. In Labov's
(1966:6-7) words:

      It is generally considered that the
most consistent and coherent system is that
of an idiolect... According to this view, as
we consider the speech of [any] individual
over longer periods, or the combined dialects
of a neighborhood, a town, or a region, the
system becomes progressively more inconsis-
tent....
      The present study adopts an entirely
opposite view...in New York City, most idiolects do not form a simple, coherent system:
on the contrary, they are studded with oscil-
lations and contradictions....
      Traditional dialect studies have shown
that isolation leads to linguistic diversity,
while the mixing of populations leads to
linguistic uniformity. Yet in the present
study of a single speech community, we will
see a new and different situation: groups
living in close contact are participating
in rapid linguistic changes which lead to
increased diversity, rather than uniformity.
      Our understanding of this apparent
paradox stems from the recognition that the
most coherent linguistic system is that which
includes the...speech community as a whole.

(Cf. also Labov 1972b:109.)
While there have been scholars working in the
same general framework as Bloomfield and Bloch, e.g.
Gleason (1961:392), who have conceded the worth of
what Saussure called secondary studies of external

linguistic phenomena, the lack of an impressive pro-
ject in this direction argues for the limitations of
their orientation. Less than twenty years ago Hockett
(1955:14) was once willing to relegate semantics and
phonetics, the two poles which grammars are supposed
to link, to the subsidiary roles of "peripheral subsystems".[6]
    The positivist rejection of universals and the
empiricist rejection of abstract explanations in the
pre-transformational orientation are uncompromisingly
stated by Joos (1966:96).

> ...in the long run [Praguean] ideas
> were not found to add up to an adequate
> methodology [sic]. Trubetzkoy phonology
> tried to explain everything from articu-
> latory acoustics [sic] and a minimum set
> of phonological laws taken as essentially
> valid for all languages alike, flatly
> contradicting the American (Boas) tra-
> dition that languages could differ from
> each other without limit and in unpre-
> dictable ways, and offering too much of
> a phonological explanation where a sober
> taxonomy would serve as well.
>   Children want explanations, and there
> is a child in each of us; descriptivism
> makes a virtue of not pampering that child.

    The advent of Noam Chomsky signaled a swing of the
pendulum to the opposite extreme of idealism or rationalism, a climate favorable to universals and unfavor-
able to unpredictability. Chomsky not only countered
the positivist position with a seeking for universals,
which had already been mooted by Roman Jakobson and
Joseph Greenberg, but also checked taxonomy with an
insistence on explanation. He countered behaviorism
with mentalism, and empiricism with abstract underlying
representations. And a newer, conceptualist orientation
is now accepting naturalness as the basis of both explanation and prediction.[7]
    Following Jakobson, Chomsky and Morris Halle pro-
moted a broadening of the restrictions on the analysis
of variation which went at least one degree beyond mere
phonic and morphic complementarity. For they made

morphophonic relationships the underlying representations of phonological analysis, paralleling abstract
representations in syntactic analysis. But those in
the transformational school were not willing to endorse
further broadening to provide abstract underlying representations for transtylistic and transpersonal variants
in whole language systems. This was so even though it
is part of speakers' knowledge of their language to use
different styles and part of hearers' knowledge to communicate with speakers employing different variants of
the language system from their own. Although for opposite reasons, Chomsky endorsed the Blochian view of
interstylistic and interpersonal variation. His
strongly Saussurian attitude is clear in this statement by him of the doctrine of homogeneity (1965:3-4):

> Linguistic theory is concerned pri-
> marily with an ideal speaker-listener, in a
> completely homogeneous speech-community, who
> knows its language perfectly and is unaf-
> fected by such grammatically irrelevant con-
> ditions as [performance variations]. This
> seems to me to have been the position of the
> founders of modern general linguistics, and
> no cogent reason for modifying it has been
> offered.

Whatever mental property enables children to internalize grammars can be just as adequately and more easily
discovered from homogeneous data as it can from complex
heterogeneous data. What language-users know about the
function of their language, including their ability
competently to communicate with speakers having different grammars, is to be investigated in secondary studies
of performance. Formal grammatical competence is inadequate to account for anything but the imaginary
desert-island situation.[8]
    While the simplifying idealization advocated by
Chomsky has probably been a necessary step in the
development toward an adequate theory of language,
sociolinguists, variationists, and generative semanticists maintain that even formal grammatical competence
has to include the functional knowledge of how to communicate. Their Platonic abstraction of idealized essences from the fluctuation of phenomena has not

prevented Chomsky and Halle (1968:49,54) from believing that different varieties of a language have
many 'early' rules in common. The idealistic orientation thus permits a degree of abstraction which
paradoxically embraces more empirical variants than
what linguists of the empiricist persuasion allow.
    The interests of some linguists who appear to
subscribe to the homogeneity doctrine have led them
to a concern with how understanding occurs among different varieties of a language. The early attempt of
Klima 1964 discussed rules and different orderings of
rules for converting one grammar to another. Such
grammars could represent different styles of a single
speaker. Rules like Klima's, variously known as
extension, linking, shifting, and conversion rules,
have been defended in Butters 1971, where they are
accorded status in competence, and in Agard 1971.
Troike's (1969) generative diaphonemic rules are not
thought of as part of language-users' competence.
In a study of Black Vernacular English (hereafter
BVE), Loflin 1971 (the relevant paragraph is absent
in earlier versions of this writing) proposed that
language varieties with similar deep structures are
related by means of low-level rules belonging to a
special 'component'. Houston (1970:11) speaks in
favor of contingency rules, which belong to systematic performance, "are quantificational in the
sense that they are marked for general probability
of occurrence in a particular way", and convert a
"basic competence" into "dialect forms, into regis-
tral forms, and into the regular patterns of idiolect...."
    The issue that has been the concern of these
writers and the variationists revolves around the
inevitable differences among even speakers of the
same 'dialect'.[9] The Chomskian teaching that that
universal mental property, the faculté de langage,
can be sufficiently discovered with restricted and
invariant data is the basis for obviating the otherwise contradictory character of these two observations: (1) the non-universal character of an idiolect
within a language system; (2) the futility and unre-
warding nature of investigating all the idiolects of
a language. Elliott, Legum, and Thompson (1969:52)
have justly scored the attitude towards data

differences that has prevailed, which they have summed
up in the words, "You describe your dialect, I'll describe mine." This procedure has not prevented such
linguists from basing universal conclusions on data
that are not even universal for the population of a
single classroom. Finally, it falls something short
of professionalism to refer to isolated differences as
'dialectal', in view of the traditional notion of dialects as mutually intelligible varieties of a language
separated by bundles of covarying phenomena, even if
this notion is hardly a useful or serviceable one.

      It will be worth reflecting that, if an inter-
personal dialect is as simple an abstraction as this
procedure and Bloch's previously mentioned definition
imply, it poses fewer analytical problems than an
internalized interstylistic grammar that generates all
the (competence) variants in an individual language-
user's language. There are amply attested languages
in which allegro-tempo neutralizations result in fewer
vowels or consonants in rapid tempos and informal
styles than in slower tempos and formal styles.[10] In
actual fact, interstylistic and interpersonal differences are quite comparable in terms of writing grammars that generate both, as linguists must do if they
are to account for language-users' knowledge of their
language. Labov 1966 and much subsequent work have
provided evidence that some class differences among
different speakers covary with and are equivalent to
style differences in the usage of the members of a
single class. This being so, Loflin's suggestion already referred to would require a special 'component'
for shifting from the grammar used in one style to
that used in another.

      It should also be clear that the same difficulties
are posed by abstracting from idiolects[11] to dialects
as by abstracting from dialects to languages; so why
not formulate grammars of entire languages that generate all their subvarieties and be more comprehensive?[12]

      This rather obvious point was made more than
eighty-five years ago by Hugo Schuchardt (1971:M-14),
who happens to have been a creolist as well as dia-
lectologist: "...therefore everything which is valid
of the relationship between dialects of any level has
to be valid also of that between idiolects...." Schuchardt was clear that every form of speech is a transitional sort of thing, and he knew that the closer you

get to the individual, the more you will find deviations from the regularity of the overall system.
Both points have been amply confirmed in recent research.

If one has read the writings of the pioneers of
Romance dialect geography or taken a look, for example,
at the data of the North of England (cf. Kolb 1966 and
see Fig. 10, pg. 87, or if one has considered the failure of structuralist attempts to make the term dialect
meaningful, one will have difficulty accepting the traditional characterization of a dialect, as set forth
above. Isoglosses do not usually bundle in a neat manner without a great deal of fudging, including the
ignoring of overlaps at the boundaries of phenomena
which are mostly located in different parts of the map;
everyone speaks transitional dialects (cf. Weinreich et
al., 184), to use traditional terminology without imply-
ing the existence of varieties of language which are
not transitional in the sense being considered. Linguistically adjacent varieties of a language are fre-
quently dispersed in spatial mappings, which detracts
from the utility of such maps for formulating grammars
of entire languages. If cross-hatchings of class, sex,
age, and other social differences are superimposed on
maps of regional variation (for some given combination
of social parameters), the traditional notion of dialect becomes hopelessly inadequate and at war with
reality[13] And the criterion of mutual intelligibility,
long known to be of little use, loses all pretenses to
validity if (Bailey 1972) speakers of marked phenomena
are able to understand speakers of unmarked phenomena
with greater readiness than conversely. An alternative to dialects will be proposed later in §2.1.

In what follows, the terms lect and isolect will
be employed in place of dialect. Lect is a completely
non-commital term for any bundling together of linguistic phenomena[14] Isolects are varieties of a language
that differ only in a minimal way, say by the presence
or weighting (see §3.1) of a single feature in a rule,
or by a minimal difference in rule ordering. A single
isogloss stands between two isolects of a language.

In view of what has been said, it should be clear
that the time has come to abandon the previously orthodox view that language-users have competence only in
their own 'dialect'. The view stated several years ago
by Becker (1968:7) was:

> Whenever a rule is found in more
> than one dialect, it must be remembered
> that its presence is motivated entirely
> by the requirements placed on the form of
> a generative phonology and the data of the
> dialect in question. No attempt has been
> made to set up common underlying forms for
> the three dialects. The independence of
> the three phonologies presented here cannot
> be over-emphasized, for without it this
> [writing] could be construed to be not a
> synchronic phonological study, but rather
> a kind of exercise in the application of
> the comparative method of historical lin-
> guistics to some closely related German
> dialects.

The object of the following sections is precisely
to demonstrate that the dichotomy between the diachronic and synchronic approaches just suggested is a
misguided one, and that children do indeed possess the
reconstructive and comparative methods of internalizing
what they know of their language and its variations--
knowledge that extends beyond their own 'idiolects'.
While I am not contending that diachronic and synchronic
studies are the same thing, I am contending, and have
given reasons (in Bailey 1972) for believing, that
their essential methods are the same. We need no longer
feel guilty, as Bloomfield may have when he realized
that his avowedly descriptive analysis of Menomini
[1939(1964):106] looked like a historical analysis.
As the Saussurian point of view won acceptance,
fewer dissentient voices were raised, and the Saussurian
paradox prevailed. Labov (1972b:105) expresses this
paradox as follows:

> The social aspect [langue] of language
> can be studied through the intuitions of any
> one individual, while the individual aspect
> [parole] can be studied only by sampling
> the behavior of an entire population.

But perhaps a discerning reader will suppose that
the writer has fallen into a paradox of his own. On
the one hand, I have maintained that the structuralists

and transformationalists, in their insistence on the
homogeneity of their descriptions, have abstracted
too far away from the data; on the other hand, I have
implied that grammars ought to abstract beyond the
idiolectal level to a much higher and more abstract
transpersonal level. The apparent paradox evaporates
when it is seen that my position is one in which it is
maintained that, whatever the level of abstraction
represented by a grammar may be, it should contain
underlying representations and rules which will generate all the systematic variation in the data at the
systematic phonetic level of every lect abstracted
from. Thus the abstract and empirical issues are re-
solved without slighting either.

1.2 The temporal paradox. One of Saussure's most
memorable statements asserted that it is the "time
factor" that causes linguistic differentiation
(Saussure 1962:271 = 1959:198). Continuing, he says:
"Geographical diversity ought to be thought of as
temporal diversity." One could go further and say
that diversity in social space ought to be thought of
as a function of the time factor. Social space is
divided by the barriers of space, age, sex, and
classes (whether based on birth, occupation, economic
status, educational attainment, ethnic or religious
background, future aspiration, etc.) and whatever
social factors determine different styles of speaking,
whether the status of the interlocutors or the lofti-
ness of the subject. New phenomena begin--at first
variably and in limited linguistic environments--in
some corner of social space defined by the conjunction
of values for each sociological parameter. In the
manner prescribed by the wave model and accompanying
sociolinguistic algorithms (see §§4.1,4), the change
spreads in time from one adjacent set of social characteristics to the next and from more restricted to
more general linguistic environments. The effects of
time are seen in the order of change and in the resulting patterns. (Cf. also Weinreich et al., 155.)
     Saussure, an Indo-Europeanist of the very first
calibre, began with the good intention of ridding language descriptions of an atomistic approach and of
historically valid, but psychologically invalid, analyses. If his notion of langue counteracted his social

view of language, his good intentions for arriving at
psychologically valid formulations also issued in
what I hope to show in the following section is a psychologically invalid result. The attempt artificially
to freeze language data and ignore the on-going nature
of linguistic change has forced linguists into strait-
jacketed descriptions which exclude a vast amount of
linguistic knowledge or language-user competence, including the elemental facts of a grandchild's communicating with his grandparent. Erecting walls between
descriptive, historical, and dialectological pursuits
has proved a cure worse than the disease. Aside from
the untoward effects on linguistic description, there
has been an unfortunate trichotomization of the discipline into pursuits which have been theoretically
more or less isolated from one another, while logic
and the study of the use of language have been dele-
teriously excluded altogether. Bloomfieldian behaviorism went further and excluded the study of presupposition and force (or intention) from syntax.

     Since Saussure's view of synchronic analysis led
him to refer to that pursuit as static linguistics,
this term will be retained in what follows. But
dynamic linguistics will be preferred to his term for
the pursuit of diachronic analysis--evolutive linguistics. To quote Saussure:

          It is therefore an [inner] necessity
     that compels us to split up linguistics into
     two parts, each having its own principle.
     [1962:115 = 1959:79]
          The opposition between the two view-
     points--synchronic and diachronic--is absolute
     and allows of no compromise. [1962:119 =
     1959:83]
          ...diachronic facts quite obviously
     have no relationship to the static fact that
     they have produced; they are of a different
     order. [1962:120 = 1959:83]
          So a diachronic fact is an event that
     has its raison d'être in itself: the particu-
     lar synchronic results that may devolve from
     it are entirely separate from it. [1962:121 =
     1959:84]
          This essential difference between suc-
     cessive terms and co-existent terms, between

partial facts and facts affecting the system, precludes making [both] the ones and
the others the matter of a single science.
[1962:124 = 1959:87]
          ...despite certain contrary appear-
ances, diachronic events always have an
accidental and particular character.
[1962:131 = 1959:93]
          The radical antinomy between dynamic
[évolutif] and static fact has the result
that all the notions relating to the one or
the other are equally irreducible to one
another...So it is that the synchronic
'phenomenon' has nothing in common with the
diachronic...the one is a relation among
simultaneous elements; the other, the sub-
stitution of one element for another in
time--a [metalinguistic?] event.
[1962:129 = 1959:91]

The thought world of his time forced Saussure
into thinking of change as a succession of states.[15]
His view that only states matter presupposes a con-
trariety between descriptive science and time. Since
Saussure's death, new outlooks have made the absence
of a relationship between past cause and present result anything but the obvious thing it seemed to that
scholar. Even on such terms, ignoring historicism and
the work of Einstein, how can linguists overlook the
manner in which language-users competently communicate
across temporally caused differences? It was already
obvious to Schuchardt in 1885 that "the old and the
new appear distributed within a dialect, however, not
only according to age, but also according to sex, edu-
cation, temper--in short, in most diverse ways" (M-15).
Indeed, this is the basis for saying that "every stage
of a language is a transitional stage, each as normal
as any other..." (M-18). Schuchardt also refers to
Karl Brugmann's assumption that mother and daughter
forms could exist side by side not only in a given dialect, but even within one and the same individual. If
what was obvious to Schuchardt eighty-five years ago
is even more palpable today, there should be no doubt
that a Newtonian or non-temporal linguistic framework
is as inadequate for linguistics as pre-Einsteinian
frameworks are for physics. So, however much one may

fault the Neo-Grammarians for their view of change
and for their family-tree model, one must acknowledge
that they worked within a temporal framework.

Occasional dissent from the Saussurian dichotomy
between static and dynamic linguistics was lost in the
prevailing climate, sometimes because appropriate
models for implementing a different theory were not
provided by the dissenters, sometimes because of fail-
ures to motivate other points of view with adequate
justification on the metatheoretical level against
Saussurianism, and sometimes because of simple mis-
understandings. In his Oslo Report, Jakobson (1958)
denied that 'statics' and synchrony coincide in linguistics any more than in physics. Jakobson (24)
phrased the matter as follows:

> Permanence, statics in time, becomes a
> pertinent problem of diachronic linguistics,
> while dynamics, the interplay of subcodes
> within the whole of a language, grows into a
> crucial question of linguistic synchrony.

Jakobson's ideas on these topics had more influence on
his followers in the social sciences than on linguists.
Linguistics did not develop the necessary models for
carrying out analysis within a dynamic framework within
the decade following Jacobson's statement. Despite
interesting suggestions, the situation in linguistics
up to a couple of years ago had been accurately described in the following words of LePage (1966:vi-vii):

> It is now being recognized that this
> division [sc. between synchronic and diachronic
> studies] helps to falsify the picture. The
> descriptive analysis of an idiolect at any
> given moment may reveal a great many over-
> lapping systems, some of which are coming to
> the end of a period of change, others just
> beginning. The descriptive analyst freezes
> for a moment what is in fact a highly dynamic
> system, and describes it in static terms. The
> 'quantum mechanics' era in linguistics has not
> yet arrived, but I believe that the study of
> Creole languages will help it forward....
>   Many of the world's languages have prob-
> ably undergone some degree of creolization at

> one time or another; by studying what is
> happening under our noses at the present
> day we should get a much better idea of
> what has happened...in the past. Until we
> have evolved descriptive techniques some-
> what analogous to those of quantum mechanics,
> however, the best we can do is to describe
> the two ends of the linguistic spectrum...
> and give some indication of the continuum in
> between.

The aim of the present undertaking is to show that
LePage's words are no longer true, that the future
framework he envisioned in 1966 is in fact now being
realized.

In the vast community of all who communicate
fluently and competently with one another in English,
changes will be more advanced among younger speakers
than among older ones. Men lag almost a generation
behind women of the same sociological description
in some instances (Labov 1972b:118). Changes beginning in informal styles and in the lower classes will
reach the upper class formal style much later, etc.

Describing the competence of such speakers in
formulations representing the internalized grammars
which generate all the differences with which they
deal competently is impossible with static models.
The artificially idealized data which they handle
represent but fragments of language-users' competence,
which is distorted when forced into such procrustean
moulds. At the very least (Bailey 1972), we must
attribute to language-users an internalized comparative
method.

Saussure himself admitted (1962:113 = 1959:78)
that "if time is excluded, the reality of language is
not complete...". Unlike Chomsky, he realized that
his methodological simplification was something of a
distortion. This makes even more perplexing his contention that the synchronic viewpoint is the only
reality for the community of speakers. Indeed, Saussure himself had the insight at one point to state the
temporal paradox (1962:113 = 1959:78) as follows:

> If you took langue in time, apart from the
> mass of speakers--suppose an isolated individual
> living through several centuries--you would

> perhaps not establish any change; time
> would produce no result in it. Conversely,
> if you considered the mass of speakers apart
> from time, you would not see the effect of
> the social forces that operate on langue.

It was the fear of time that led to antipathy
toward processes in structuralism, and eventually to
a baffling preference for lists of allomorphs over
generalized rules for morphophonic relationships.
While operating fully within the static framework,
Chomsky & Halle (331) at least admit that the notion
of instantaneous acquisition of language by children
is a counterfactual simplification.[16] Now that dynamic models which were not available to them in the
sixties have become available, their statement that a
non-instantaneous model of acquisition would be too
complex is no longer relevant. In more general terms,
it is worth stressing that there is no reason whatever to suppose that simplified static models would
ever prove adequate for the real-life situation in
which language is used, although, on the other hand,
a more complex time-based theory would work as well
for the imaginary desert-island situation as for the
real-life one.
    Static models are also inadequate for dealing
with diachronic linguistics. Some transformationalists (e.g. Kiparsky MS) have sought to bring unity
into their work by testing synchronic models with
attested historical changes, although there is still a
reluctance to allow performance to influence competence
(notwithstanding the admission that one purpose of
transformations is to make abstract underlying representations performable).[17] And yet the gradual (variable) initiation of changes, well-documented (e.g.
Labov 1966) among variationists, has generally not been
incorporated into the transformationalists' overall
theory of change.[18] The doctrine that grammars are
monolectal is seen within the perspective of the gradual initiation of change to contradict the doctrine
that linguistic changes are changes of rules, i.e. of
significant linguistic generalizations. (See Kiparsky
1971, which provides a popular summary of more tech-
nical writings by Halle, Paul Postal, and himself.)
This can be shown with a simple example.

In the Western States, the sound which is [ɔ]
in many other varieties of English began to be heard
as [ɑ], first in paroxytones like naughty, where an
apical followed the nucleus; then in oxytones like
caught and dawn, where an apical also follows the
nucleus; and finally, speakers are now introducing
[ɑ] (or failing to change underlying //ɒ// to [ɔ])
before velars, as in hawk. The result of the changes
is to make the words cited sound like notty, cot, don,
and hock, respectively. Younger speakers are of course
more advanced in the change than older speakers. We
may further assume, on the basis of what is known of
other examples of change, that the oldest speakers have
[ɑ] in the oldest environment, an alternation between
formal [ɔ] and allegro [ɑ] in the next-oldest environment, and only unchanged [ɔ] in the prevelar one; and
that the youngest speakers have only [ɑ] in the two
oldest environments, but an alternation between formal
[ɔ] and allegro [ɑ] in the newest one. A monolectal
phonology can show only one of the vowels in single-
style grammars; where both vowels appear in a single
style, if they should do so, the most that can be shown
is an equipollent (unweighted and non-directional)
optionality between them. When the new pronunciation
of naughty (like notty) is first introduced (borrowed)
into a speaker's language, it is not of course a rule
generalization, but only a relexification, since the
new [ɑ] cannot be 'compared' with older [ɔ] in some
other style or in the language of some other group in
the speech community without contradicting the premises
of the monolectal doctrine. Unless a sizable number of
new [ɑ] pronunciations are introduced on the same day,
the likelihood of a new generalization's being internalized is vanishingly small. Hence, the two fundamental
doctrines of change in transformationalism combine to
make change impossible. The paradox is obviated in the
polylectal grammars of the variationist framework, since
the vector-like models employed there formalize language-
users' knowledge both of new and old forms in their own
different styles and in the different class and other
lects with which they communicate competently.

Note that whatever relations language-users may in-
fer about the variants that they become familiar with
will no doubt tell them something (and something that
is correct in many instances) about the history of their

language. Given 'natural' effects of natural developments in history, the <u>uniformitarian principle</u>
which is accepted in historical sciences like geology
should also apply in such instances (Labov 1972b:
101,MS). There will, nevertheless, be differences
in historical and descriptive analysis. As noted in
Bailey 1972, what may be only exceptions in the latter
may prove to be valuable relics in the former.

The effects of current studies of creolization on
historical analysis have already been alluded to above
and outlined in Bailey 1973a. The prevalence of creolization, especially as an important means of introducing 'unnatural' or 'marked' phenomena into a language system, is becoming more widely recognized[19]
Since creolization may be the only means by which new
language systems can arise, it seems more than probable
that every system or node in a family tree should have
at least two parents. Even so, the family-tree model
will have a more doubtful status in future analyses
than in former ones.

There is an additional static paradox, but discussion of it will have to be postponed to §4.1.

2 THE NEW FRAMEWORK

2.0 <u>General observations</u>. To review the substance
of Bailey 1971, the new framework advocated by the
writer has two aspects, corresponding to §§1.1,2
which have just preceded. Its ideological <u>orienta-
tion</u> contrasts with the homogeneity doctrine of both
positivism and rationalism. My orientation is the
traditional and perennial one of <u>conceptualism</u>, which
accepts as real and worthy of study both the flux of
variation in data (in contrast with Platonism, idealism, and rationalism) and also the reality and suit-
ability for study of abstract relations among data
variants (as opposed to positivism and empiricism).
The second aspect of the new framework is the <u>dynamic
paradigm</u>, which, in contrast with the static paradigm
of both structuralism and transformationalism, includes time as a fundamental dimension of all analysis.
     To allay any misunderstandings about conceptual
bias, it should be stressed that my orientation is not
the essentialist conceptualism of western scholasticism,
but the vitalist conceptualism of post-Hellenistic
scholasticism. The former concentrates on essences
and ignores life and function, which the Greek scholasticism emphasizes above all. But all scholastic
argumentation involves tightly-knit logical arguments
which begin and end in data--empirical data, if the
question is an empirical one. It is important to
stress this, in order to characterize the position being taken here vis-à-vis the new empiricism cropping up
in sociolinguistic and glottometric circles, where
<u>scholastic</u> is a term of opprobrium. The acceptance of
abstract hypotheses and formalized arguments does not
commit me to any acceptance of Platonic views on innate
'knowledge' or the role of intuition as more than a
sometimes useful discovery tool. On the other hand, the
acceptance of naturalness in linguistics (cf. fn. 7)

does not commit me to the acceptance of statistics as
more than a sometimes useful discovery procedure. And
if it can be shown that theory is underdetermined by
data (as it can), it can also be shown that (inadequate)
theories of language exclude from the status of factu-
ality data that are as theoretically important to account for as the data which such theories do accept,
and therefore that data cannot be easily overincluded
in a theoretical framework.

I do not find it credible or useful to suppose
that children can internalize relative quantities as
such (cf. also Bickerton 1971), especially where cross
products like those found in most treatments of variable rules (cf. Labov 1969) are concerned. Nor do I
limit linguistic reality to the measurable. Like
probably most linguists, I have been convinced (e.g.
by Labov 1966) that relative quantities do exist in
language data, are systematic, and can be predicted.
Like other variationists, I reject the idea that language-users' demonstrated ability to interpret and produce the statistics is a matter of 'performance' rather
than of basic linguistic competence. But I disagree
with glottometrists in that it is not the statistics
which are acquired, learned, or internalized, but
rather a psychologically credible implicational pattern
generated by the wave model (§4.1).

Scholasticism at its best maintained a psychoso-
matic view of man and his nature. Man is not simply
the mind endowed with innate knowledge of the last orientation in linguistics, but also a body whose physiological characteristics define the limits of 'naturalness' in language. Man is Aristotle's communal animate
being whose 'life' is social. As the object of linguistic study, this conception of man demands the inclusion
of the function of language in its social context as an
essential part of linguistics. The scholastic balance
in these matters is further seen in the balance between
what is variable and what is constant (the emphasis of
the rationalist orientation): water : fish = air : bird.

Since linguistics, like the sciences, is an æsthetic pursuit for all but its drudges, it must seek to
preserve an æsthetic balance as well as a balance of
all sides of what is truth. One cannot overstress the
dangers of a new and doctrinaire empiricism, possibly
striving to emerge in some circles, which would denigrate

explanatory hypotheses as 'thought experiments' and
elevate methodology above theory. This will prove no
more adequate a remedy for the doctrinaire rationalism
just past than that in turn was for the older doctrinaire empiricism.

It should also be said that my position is not
that of <u>some</u> 'sociolinguists'--viz. that the study of
variation is simply a valuable adjunct to linguistics--
but rather that the study of patterned language variation in its communicative life <u>cannot be omitted from
linguistic theory and practice without invalidating
them</u>. What is proposed below is not so much a new theory as a new framework. This framework will of course
transform much that is taken over from generative theory, e.g. the study of sound relationships in phonology
will now include the level of interpersonal and interstylistic variation. Models will be provided for implementing the new point of view in terms of concrete analyses, for even good ideas remain barren without these.

2.1 <u>Justification of polylectal grammars</u>. Given the
complexity of the data on variation that will be considered, it is incumbent on anyone who would claim that
language variation belongs to competence not only to
show that language-users do in fact competently deal
with variation in the very formulation of their internalized grammars, but also to put forward credible
hypotheses concerning how the attested patterns could
be acquired by children and stored within the brain
(cf. fn. 69). One should eschew theories for which
no plausible mode of acquisition and storage can be
suggested. Indeed, the patterns of variation in language could well provide psycholinguists with interesting hypotheses concerning the structure of the brain
for profitable future investigations. What follows is
an account of the nature of children's acquisition of
language which is so basic that the writer hopes it
will be obvious and non-controversial to the reader.

Two main assumptions are being entertained in the
present account: (1) Speaking competence is a relatively small subset of the much vaster competence required for understanding those one competently communi-
cates with; and (2) a child, in an on-going process, is
constantly revising his internalized grammar with every
new encounter with systematic variation in the speech

of others, and this is done in such a way as to create
an underlying grammar which will generate all the variants that he must competently cope with. Let us now
consider what happens during the first decade of lan-
guage-acquisition, say up to the age of twelve, which
is the crucial period for acquiring native competence
in a language.

Ordinarily, a child is mostly exposed to the speech
of females in his earliest years. The child is eventually confronted with the speech of his grandparents,
who may all be from other regions. Some of them may be
of different social classes from each other and from
the child's parents. The child, of course, meets neigh-
bors of different regional backgrounds and may travel
to neighboring and distant locales. He will communicate with language-users of different classes at school,
delivering papers or mowing lawns, at shops and markets,
etc.; even in private schools children meet students
from more distant locales in compensation for the lack
of a variety of class lects, although school employees
may provide these. Since it is known that women are
about a generation ahead of men in some changes, the
language of one's mother will be different from that
of one's father, even if their age and class traits
are similar. Each of the interlocutors encountered
by a child has a multitude of styles which he or she
must competently deal with, and there is whispered
speech to cope with also in each instance. The spread
of radio and other communicational media in this century has further extended the range of data that the
child copes with.

The result is that what the child produces gets
more and more restricted to the exemplar of his peers
(unless he is isolated from them), while what he has
in his understanding competence is constantly being
enlarged. That our 'active' vocabularies are only subsets of our 'passive' ones is widely recognized. But
such considerations have not deterred educational psy-
chologists from equating competence with language production (during interviews, especially with poor children), nor linguists from trying to exhaust competence
by asking, 'Would you say...?' Klima & Bellugi 1966:
183 say: "Sentences the child understands describe the
scope of his grammar more accurately than those he produces, just as with the adult"[20]. Against Chomsky's

view of the symmetry between productive and understanding competence (cf. Shipley, Smith & Gleitman
1969:337 fn. 8), most linguists today accept the
asymmetry of the two. On children's competence, compare again the opinion of Shipley et al. (1969:336-
337):

> Our data show that children make dis-
> criminations that are not reflected in their
> speech....Thus a description of the child's
> spontaneous utterances does not do justice
> to his linguistic organization. In some
> fairly clear sense, comprehension seems to
> precede the production of well-formed sen-
> tences....A description of natural speech
> leaves this implicit system entirely out of
> account. Therefore, in no sense can recent
> descriptions of children's speech...be taken
> as <u>grammars</u> of child language.

The linguist can run around tape-recording every
utterance of his informants, but if their competence
is greater than what they produce, it follows that
such recordings, however thorough, will not exhaust,
even remotely, his informants' competence. This
does not mean that competence cannot be empirically
determined, as the work of Shipley et al. in fact
shows.
    At this juncture, it may be of service to pro-
vide a simple illustration of the reconstructive and
comparative method in the acquisition of language by
children. There have to be at least three stages:
(1) The child relates the pronunciations of words he
hears in the mouths of different speakers and inter-
nalizes a reconstructed representation from which all
of them (aside from what were earlier called performance variations) can be systematically generated in
his understanding. (2) He acquires different pronunciations for different styles with respect to many
of his underlying representations, thus broadening
his production variation. This may coincide with the
beginning of (3) the child's learning to relate different forms of morphemes in different contexts. At
first perhaps the child learns to distinguish formal
[t] from informal [d] in a word like <u>cheater</u>, related

to cheat with [t] only. Eventually this ability will
be extended to cope with more complex instances like
ignite : ignition.

It will not be doubted that variation is heard by
the child in the nucleus of came, game, save, way,
rain, laid, cane, etc., and in the slightly shorter
one in late, wait, gate, hate, etc. Of course, no two
pronunciations of the same word, even by the same
speaker, are identical. But children descend from the
more general to the less general, e.g. calling all
animals doggie before learning to distinguish the different kinds of animals. By whatever method they may
use, they identify the common internal representation
of all the variants of a word like train uttered by
different speakers with whom they come into contact;
and presumably they learn to identify the nucleus in
this word with the one in came, game, save, etc., and
even with the one in late, wait, gate, etc. It could
hardly be open to question that the underlying representation of their internalized grammars is eventually
revised to handle different pronunciations of the
nucleus which are more or less diphthongized in different environments, in which the peak will be closer or
opener or more or less retracted, etc. Other nuclei
in English exhibit even greater variety than the one
chosen here for illustrative purposes, which is relatively stable. The talents displayed in these efforts
are gradually extended to handle morphophonic variants
like sane : sanity when the child progresses to the
stage that he must cope with these.

Chomskian linguists obliquely grant that the
faculté de langage includes the ability to employ the
method of internal reconstruction in creating underlying representations like those of sane and sanity,
at least on the synchronic level. If we accept some
kind of naturalness condition that requires rules to be
of the sort that could evolve in real historical change,
then we must conclude that children have within them
the ability to 'reconstruct' history in some sense (cf.
Chafe 1970:7). For the dimension of history is spread
out synchronically on the other dimension of lectal
differentiation, just as a beam of white light which
has passed through a prism spreads out in a rainbow on
a surface perpendicular to the beam. Given the possible
restructurings, generalizations, and the like which can

change the structures of past times to different ones
later on, the reconstructions of the child will not
exactly coincide with those the linguist reconstructs
with the help of earlier records. The child who has
never heard the Irish pronunciations of mean and meant
will hardly assign these and similar words the same
underlying vowel that he assigns to break : breakfast
and retain : retention. But, just as the historical
linguist can reconstruct a parent tongue from the
residue in either a few unleveled[21] scions or a larger
number of leveled ones, so the child can asymptotically
approach a panlectal competence in his language and a
grammar that resembles the same one that other users of
the language are also asymptotically approaching from
somewhat different data, or at least data encountered
in a somewhat different sequence. The ability of
language-users to do this argues for their possession
of the 'comparative method'. So far from agreeing with
Kiparsky (1971:310) that "the child is the synchronic
linguist par excellence", I would say: "The child is
the comparatist par excellence!"
     What distinguishes the view of language being pre-
sented here from static, homogeneous views of language
is that the goal of acquiring a language to communicate
is taken seriously and treated as the fundamental consideration in trying to understand language. The account just given clearly accepts the requirement of
justifying grammars on the basis of what is psychologically plausible or provable[22] Without this con-
straint, of course, there would be no bounds to combining the most diverse data into a single, supposedly
unified, putative 'system'. The grammar envisioned in
these pages is not located in some reified 'communal
mind', socially real though the grammar is claimed to
be. And it certainly does not presuppose two compe-
tences, one for speaking and one for understanding,
despite some asymmetry between the subset and the overall set. The naturalness criterion provides further
constraints (which are quite strong) on the kinds of
formulations that are tolerated.
     It should be obvious that a polylectal grammar can
be a psychologically real one, even though no single
language-user has all of it internalized, if every pair
of adjacent subsystems which are attested are unified
in some language-user's internalized competence. In

such a case, there is no risk in positing that the
whole grammar is potentially internalizable for a
given language-user exposed to all the subsystems of
the language.

Until now, the discussion has omitted an additional factor relating to competence, viz. literacy.
That literacy greatly affects competence and one's
underlying representations can scarcely be doubted,
despite all the insistence by modern linguists on the
spoken form of a language, but psycholinguists have
been negligent in providing linguists with an adequate
account of these effects. Speakers who do not hesi-
tate to pronounce Einstinian (the adjective for
Einstiné) with [ɪ] in the second syllable balk at
Einsteinian, pronouncing it now with[a$(^e)$], now with
[ɪ]. When I first heard ['gra^{e}sɪən], I thought the
adjective referred to the name Greis, not Grice. And
despite exceptions (which one may or may not be able
to account for, [ŋ] seems to be more frequent for
underlying //n// before orthographic 'k' and 'g' than
before 'c' or 'q' (as in Bancroft, Hancock, and ban-
quet; contrast Bankok and Bengali).

Since Decamp 1971 (delivered in 1968), Bailey
1972 (delivered in 1969), and Elliott, Legum, & Thompson 1969, it has become increasingly obvious that a
great deal of linguistic variation patterns in an
implicational manner, i.e. item d implies c, which
implies b, which in turn implies a. This is true
both of different kinds of linguistic phenomena and
of different rules, as has been shown (cf. Bailey
1973b); it is inescapable for the suboutputs of variable rules, as will be shown later in connection with
the wave model. And even though language-users may
greatly differ in their intuitive ratings of the acceptability of different examples, they will generally
agree in the relative acceptability of the examples.

Insofar as lects differ in terms of phenomena
which can be placed on an implicational scale, they
can be uniquely designated by the point at which they
occur on such scales. The phenomenon whose presence
or absence characterizes them implies the presence or
absence of other phenomena lower on the scale and is
implied by, but does not imply, phenomena located
higher up on the scale. On-going work indicates that
the different phonologies of English can be uniquely

designated in this manner. If future work continues
to corroborate the surmise that all varieties of English can be designated in terms of a larger overall
scale including semantic and syntactic as well as phonological materials, then linguistics will have a prac-
tical concept which will prove far more serviceable than
dialect.[23] On the other hand, if sets of rules operate
in blocs vis-à-vis the rest of the rules in an implicational scaling, as suggested in Bailey 1972, perhaps
forming separate branches on an implicational scaling,
then the concept of a dialect may be amenable to being
rehabilitated, though on entirely new terms. To the
extent that implicational patterning obtains among the
lects of a language system, the polylectal system can
be formulated so as to include all the phenomena of the
system. The implicational ordering of the rules will
indicate which lects have which phenomena, while lexical features designating the lects (implicationally)
will have to handle the listings of the lexicon. Rules
will have to be formulated in the least general form in
which they are found anywhere in the language system
(Bailey 1972), the formulation will employ the most
marked feature weighting found anywhere in the system,
and whatever marked orders are found in the system will
appear in the overall grammar. Other patterns in the
system due to more general rules or to less marked
weightings of features or orderings of rules will be
generated with the principles in later sections. These
will specify how waves spread through the system and
which feature in a rule will reweight or be deleted to
make the rule more general. They will also deal with
the hierarchy of markedness,[24] the hierarchy of unmarked
feature weightings and the rules or conventions[25] that
unmark features.

2.2 Pragmatic competence. That the knowledge of how to
use one's grammar should be considered part and parcel
of one's linguistic competence, rather than performance,
has been proclaimed for a decade by Dell Hymes (cf. 1962)
and other scholars of language in the social disciplines.
The idea ran too much counter to the prevailing ethos in
linguistics, however, and for many years fell mostly on
deaf ears. But pioneering work represented by Gordon
and G. Lakoff 1971 and R. Lakoff 1972 made it clear
that competence in the use of language in social

situations has direct and perceptible effects on grammars. The leadership of these scholars and their colleagues has effected a reversal in the prevailing attitude toward what Charles Morris (1946:219) called pragmatics, viz. "that portion of semiotic which deals with the origin, uses, and effects of signs within the behavior in which they occur". Hymes' term for an equally broad area of study, which extends beyond the purely verbal, is the ethnography of communication. Those who limit attention to verbal language may wish to think of formal grammatical competence and pragmatic or functional competence as subsets of communicative competence. Formal competence refers to the substance of the grammar;[26] pragmatic competence, to the life and use of the grammar. Today there is no need to refer studies of the function of the grammar to Saussure's 'external linguistics', to studies of performance, and the like. Just as semantics has recently become the chief concern of current linguistic research of the highest degree of sophistication, it is only the natural consequence of this concern to formulate the relationship between presupposition and intention with syntactic form. Bloomfield himself (1933:141-2) was aware of the connection when he observed that a beggar and a child resisting an early bedtime mean quite different things when they say, "I'm hungry". But his approach to meaning left such observations sterile. The orientational changes effected by Chomsky created a climate for studies of such questions, but the relegation of the status and other aspects of the social contexts of conversations to performance, together with the concentration on sentence grammar, prevented the burgeoning of such studies until recently. Karttunen 1968 can now be seen as a break with the prevailing orientation.

If empiricism concentrates on the matter, and rationalism on the form, of data, conceptualism (at least of the variety espoused here) focuses on the life and functioning of its object of study. The words of R. Lakoff (922) are quite at home in such a framework:

> ...we cannot stop our analysis at the
> point of superficial structure, or at the
> point of logical structure, in fact: we must
> ask in every case what the extralinguistic

context of a sentence is, what purpose it
is used for; only on that basis can we
establish whether or not sentences in two
languages are parallel.

In contrast with old-line linguists who still maintain
that social context is not relevant to 'grammar', it
is notable that Hoenigswald (1966) some time ago was
suggesting a variety of topics which belong to a
language-user's knowledge of his language. Besides
knowledge of conventional orthographies among the
literate, he mentioned cultural suppositions about
language itself, knowledge or beliefs about the
analysis of language, and a folk vocabulary referring
to speech activity. The use of puns, obscenities,
and the like differs vastly from culture to culture,
as does the role of silence in conversation and the
veneration of rhetoric and poetry. Hoenigswald mentions differing attitudes toward interpreters' skills,
the study of when and how corrections are performed
on children, and attitudes toward stuttering and
muteness.
     The advocates of the new framework consider the
study of the use of language an idea whose time has
now come. This became very evident at the First Annual
Colloquium on New Ways of Analyzing Variation in English at Georgetown University in October, 1972, and at
the Conference on Performances, Conversational Impli-
cature, and Presuppositions at the University of Texas
in March, 1973.

2.3 <u>Paradigm characteristics and contrasts</u>. While
there exist differences among those working in the new
framework, there are a number of more or less novel
assumptions being accepted by various linguists today
which it may be helpful to list here[27].
     1. The introduction of directional vectors into
linguistic descriptions was proposed as long ago as
1949 by Fries and Pike (see the quotation in §3.0); and
later Labov (1966:10) envisioned grammars showing directionality and rate[28]. The following sections claim to
offer models for implementing such suggestions. The
models are dynamic or time-based and suitable for either
historical or descriptive analysis. They therefore
qualify as models for a view of linguistic analysis in

which historical, descriptive, and variational analysis
are integrated. They presuppose that <u>the function of
time in defining synchronic language patterns cannot
be ignored in valid descriptions of language</u>.

2. Although virtually every writer since Hermann
Paul except Saussure (1962:281,288 = 1959:205,210) has
correlated diversification of language with a reduction
in contact density and homogenization with an increase
in density, Labov's more informed view (quoted in §1.1)
is now accepted. Fishman's (1971:70) recent summariza-
tion of what has been learned on the matter concludes
that "both uniformation and differentiation are found
to go on simultaneously...".

3. The sufficiency of idiolectal data for systematic analysis is not accepted; rather <u>the grammar that
represents what speakers know about their language includes both all that they deal competently with in understanding the language of others and their ability to
vary the use of their grammar in different social con-
texts</u>. A grammar of production competence and limited
to sentences is but a subset of language-users' overall
knowledge of their language, which includes what speakers intend when they utter a sentence in an actual dis-
course. The goal of the new work is to formulate
psychologically valid polylectal grammars of language
systems.

4. One of Labov's most important contributions to
the data side of linguistic research has been ascertaining that <u>unmonitored speech is vastly more</u> systematic than monitored speech (Labov 1972b:112). The
commutation or minimal-pair test has been shown in some
instances to falsify the facts of competence (see Labov
1972b:101 fn. 3, 103). It of course goes against the
grain of long-standing (Fries & Pike 1949:35-6) assumptions to say that speakers are not consciously aware
of distinctions consistently made by them, or that
speakers lose these in monitored production, but such
is the case. The intuitive source of data which has
dominated the last orientation is obviously no longer
to be regarded per se as a reliable or valid source.

5. <u>Linguistic changes begin variably in relatively
restricted environments</u>, being later extended--at first
variably--to more general environments if the vitality
of the rule continues long enough, and eventually becoming categorical in all the environments where vari-

able.[29] Three stages are described in Weinreich et
al. (184): (1) a speaker learns an alternative form;
(2) old and new forms exist side by side within his
competence; and (3) the older form becomes obsolete.
Because most rules have long existed in any language
except a recent ex-pidgin, they will have had time to
become categorical (i.e. non-variable). Consequently,
few of the rules in a language will be variable at any
given time. Variable rules usually have sociolinguistic significance for reasons that will become clear
later.

   6. _A description of polylectal competence presupposes internal reconstruction and some comparative
method_. Given natural rules and natural modifications
of them, it should not surprise the descriptivist if
his polylectal formulation bears strong resemblances
to historical developments which in fact took place.
He will not be able to use information from the past,
however available to the philologist, when it is not
available to an illiterate child acquiring his or her
language; and he will have to treat as pure exceptions
relic relationships like that exhibited in draw : dray :
drag : draft.

   7. The prevalence of creolization in the creation
of new systems (nodes in a genealogical tree) makes
vines more likely candidates as models of intersystem
relations. In short, creoles and the utility of the
wave model make family trees obsolete. While there
are some parallels between mixing of the sybsystems
of a system and the mixing of different systems--both
result in neutralizations--much further study is necessary to determine how the two kinds of mixing differ.
There is every reason to believe that mixing of subsystems will not destroy the character (e.g. the implicational relations) of the overall system to any large
extent, while mixing systems creates new systems. The
new framework demands that the omnipresence of on-going
change be built into linguistic descriptions. In addition to the usual ways in which subsystems are differentiated within a system--the natural developments of
rule generalization, feature reweighting, and changes
from marked to unmarked rule ordering--there is the
additional process occurring in Swahili. After Swahili,
itself a creole (like probably all languages, and certainly English),[30] was further creolized with different

forms of Bantu as it spread away from the coast to
inland villages, these local creoles began to decreolize[31] in the direction of coastal Swahili, creating new lects within the system of Swahili.

The following tabulation of contrasts between
the static (whether structuralist or transformation-
alist in orientation) and dynamic paradigms is added
here to help pinpoint the differences which justify
speaking of a new paradigm:

Static Paradigm:

Dynamic Paradigm:

1. Variation other than
morphophonic variation is
to be relegated to the
category of performance and
excluded from the work of
the descriptivist.

1. If variation above
the level of systematic
phonetics is structured
and can reliably be
attributed to what lan-
guage-users know about
their language, it must
be formulated in an
adequate grammar.

2. Creole situations are
freak situations; creoles
are necessarily unstable
and rapidly changing.

2. Creolization is normal;
all languages have pro-
bably once been creoles.

3. Homogeneity is a necessary and useful fiction
that will not vitiate linguistic theory or analysis.

3. Homogeneity would be
dysfunctional in language;
sweeping variation under
the rug is deleterious to
theory and analysis.

4. Relations among different grammars can be ade-
quately portrayed with the
family tree model.

4. A wave model is re-
quired for explaining the
patterns of variation in
language data.

5. Equipollent optional
rules are sufficient to
handle all the variation
that needs to be described
in grammars that claim to
represent language-users'
competence.

5. Rules generating implicationally arranged outputs
are required to provide an
adequate account of lan-
guage-users' competence.

6. Descriptions of lan-
guage should be instan-
taneous and exclude
temporal correlations.

6. Directionality and
relative rate of change
can and should be incor-
porated into the descrip-
tive apparatus of grammars.

7. Idiolects are more
systematic than higher
abstractions; commutation
tests adequately reflect
language-users' knowledge
of their language.

7. Idiolects are not systematic; unmonitored pro-
duction is more systematic
than monitored production.

8. Understanding and pro-
duction are symmetrical.

8. Understanding and pro-
duction are not symmetrical.
(But cf. fn. 20.)

9. The Saussurian paradox:
competence is looked for
exclusively in the indi-
vidual, but variety is
sought in society.

9. Competence is polylectal;
what language-users know
about communicating with
others more nearly repre-
sents their language com-
petence than the subset of
this knowledge exhibited in
production.

10. Intelligibility among
different varieties of a
language depends on good
guessing, which is in turn
based on similarities.

10. Intelligibility among
different lects is predi-
cated either on their tauto-
systematicity or, in the
case of decreolizing gra-
datums, on one's internali-
zation of the algorithms
according to which related
systems are mixed.

3 DIRECTIONALITY AND RATE IN VARIATION

3.0 <u>Directionality and markedness</u>. While restructurings can and sometimes do occur, it remains true
that the patterns of a language are the cumulative
result of natural, unidirectional changes, which begin
variably and spread across the social barriers of age,
sex, class, space, and the like in waves. Such is the
thesis of the present writing. It is time that differ-
entiates the patterns found at different points in
social space closer to or more remote from the origin
of a change. Since however the relative rate among
different aspects of a change may affect the resulting
pattern, descriptive rules must have rate factors as
well as directionality built into them. Such rate factors must be able to handle the acceleration of later
changes ahead of earlier ones.
     What is new in the present undertaking is not the
idea, but the models, and even these are mostly adapta-
tions of Labov 1969, with the exception of the general
principles in §3.2 and §4.1. Fries & Pike (1949:42)
advocated the incorporation of directionality into linguistic description more than two decades ago:

> It is impossible to give a purely syn-
> chronic description of a complex mixed system,
> at one point of time, which shows the pertinent
> facts of that system; direction of change is a
> pertinent characteristic of the system and must
> also be known if one wishes to have a complete
> description of the language as it is structurally
> constituted.

The prevailing assumptions of the static paradigm ob-
structed the hope of realizing descriptions of the sort
that were needed.
     Even the revival of interest in marking theory among

the transformationalists led merely to a more subtle
evaluation metric. They did not replace static
plusses and minuses in rules with dynamic markings[32]
whose proneness to change endows them with directionality in accordance with this fundamental premise of
the new paradigm:

    (1a)   The directionality of natural change
           is from what is more marked to what is
           less marked;

    (1b)   when two changes conflict, unmarking on
           a higher hierarchical level may over-
           rule a lower-level feature-marking pro-
           duced by the higher-level unmarking.

    A few comments on several aspects of this prin-
ciple are in order. The first is that only natural
changes are concerned; see fn. 19 for other developments. The main [x natural] source of marked values
is borrowing. The borrower of a linguistic rule, at
least if from another language system, usually acquires a more general form of the rule, as a result
of missing one of its features (cf. children).
Secondly, the changes specified by the principle do
not have to occur. The principle indicates a pro-
clivity, a directionality of change _if_ it should
occur, not a necessity that things must change. The
need to keep words apart in communication may often
obstruct natural changes, especially those that yield
neutralizations, and prevent their occurring. Finally,
the manner in which higher-level unmarkings (cf. fn. 24)
can produce lower-level marked values of features can
be illustrated with two kinds of examples. Assimilation often produces marked neutralizations, nasal vowels
in the environment of a nasal consonant and intervocalic
lenited (voiced and continuant) obstruents. Another
example comes from the reweighting of features to their
unmarked weights (see the Appendix), since a heavier-
weighted feature may unmark at the expense of marking a
lighter-weighted one. A simple example is the change
of u to ü, where heavier-weighted [grave] changes from
a marked to an unmarked value, and lighter-weighted
[rounded] changes from an unmarked to a marked value.
The role of the formalism is important[33] and an adequate
formalism would make it impossible to formulate unnatural changes. (For the change of the vowel u to ɨ

to <u>i</u>, a change formalized as [⊃ grave] with [round] remaining unmarked, see on the implicational coefficient ⊃ below.)

Given the convention of writing heavier-weighted variable features above lighter-weighted ones in the same segment, the change of $\begin{bmatrix}(m\ F_i)\\(u\ F_j)\end{bmatrix}$ to $\begin{bmatrix}(u\ F_i)\\(m\ F_j)\end{bmatrix}$ results in an overall reduction of markedness, since the single m in the output is lighter-weighted than the single m in the input[34] This is illustrated in the change of <u>u</u> to <u>ü</u> already discussed, and will be further illustrated presently. It should also be noted that the same result can be achieved by a change that simply reweights $\begin{bmatrix}m\ F_j\\u\ F_i\end{bmatrix}$ to the unmarked weighting $\begin{bmatrix}u\ F_i\\m\ F_j\end{bmatrix}$. Where the value of a feature depends on the value of that feature in an adjacent segment, the value in the segment where it is dependently defined seems to have unmarking priority over the segment in which it is independently defined in cases where both are marked. This can be illustrated with [continuant], where [= cnt] (not-minus continuant) is more usual or unmarked than [+ cnt] in the <u>special position</u> in the syllable following the nucleus[35] The expected or unmarked value of [continuant] in the next segment (which is not in a special position) will be minus if the preceding is not minus, but plus if the preceding is minus. Therefore, <u>ft</u> and <u>xt</u> following a tautosyllabic nucleus have a [u cnt] <u>t</u>, where [continuant] is contingently defined. The change from <u>fþ</u> to <u>ft</u> in Old English and some current lects is found in <u>fift(h)</u>; cf. <u>sixt(h)</u>. This change reduces the markedness of [continuant] in the segment where it is contingently defined. A change of <u>fþ</u> to <u>pt</u> would increase the markedness of [continuant] in the segment where it is independently defined, but does not occur. The change of <u>pt</u> and <u>kt</u> to <u>ft</u> and <u>xt</u> reduces the markedness of the feature in both segments and is well-known; cf. PIE *septm̥ 'seven' and *oktŏ 'eight' with modern Greek <u>eftá</u> and <u>októ</u> and with German <u>acht</u>. The change of <u>pt, kt</u> to <u>fþ, xþ</u>, which would reduce the markedness of [continuant] only in the segment in which it is independently defined, does not seem to occur. But the feature may be unmarked where contingently defined at the cost of increasing its

markedness where independently defined, as in the
change of Old English wæfs to wæps (see below for
later Old English wæsp) 'wasp', from PIE *webhsā.

A more complicated example can now be discussed,
viz. the change of sk to ks (in the derivation of Old
English āxian from āscian 'ask' or of late West Saxon
English fixas from fiscas 'fishes'), in contrast with
the apparently opposite kind of change seen in the
change of wæfs or wæps to wæsp, modern English wasp.
Since [lingual] is less marked for k than p in the
special position, but elsewhere [lingual] is more
marked for p than for k, we might expect some explanation for the different directionality of the
changes to be found in this difference. The Appendix
shows that the values of the features which differ-
entiate [s], [p], and [k] are as follows in the special
position:

[s]: [m cnt, m liq, u sul, u grv, m lng]
[k]: [M cnt, M liq, M sul, u grv, u lng]
[p]: [M cnt, M liq, M sul, u grv, m lng]

Elsewhere these values are all unmarked for [s], though
in the case of [continuant], this is only true when a
preceding postnuclear segment (or a following prenuclear one) is [- cnt], as in the cluster being considered here. And [k] and [p] are marked as follows
in the position following an immediately postnuclear
segment:

[k]: [u cnt, u liq, u sul, m grv, M lng]
[p]: [u cnt, u liq, u sul, m grv, m lng]

A calculation of the change of ps to sp in wasp results
in about the same amount of markedness in the output as
in the input, if all features were equally valued; but
the increase in the lighter features is offset by a decrease in the heavier ones, which is therefore greater
than the increase. In the change of sk to ks, what
reduction of markedness occurs is found in the lighter-
weighted features (assuming the same relative weightings as before), but is more than the increase in marking in the heavier-weighted features. On the other
hand, a putative change of ks to sk would represent a
large increase in markedness and would not be expected.
The change of sp to ps would similarly be unexpected
because it would involve at least as great an increase
of marking as decrease, and the increase would be in
the heavier, not the lighter, features. If this change

is found, it will be necessary to assume a different,
presumably marked, weighting of the feature values.

The widely attested change of tk and tp to kt
and pt, respectively, is an unmarking of [grave] in
both segments. The further change of kt, pt to tt
(e.g. Italian fatto, rotto) is an assimilatory change;
see Principle 1b above. The simplification to Spanish
roto is a feature-unmarking. What of the opposite
changes of x to f and f to x in many languages? It is
easy to assume that x would become f before a nucleus
and that f would become x following a tautosyllabic
nucleus, if their values of [lingual] correspond to
those of k and p. A crazy rule (cf. Bach and Harms
1972) could then generalize the new segment to other
environments (see further fn. 38). Similarly, the
change of apical [r] to uvular [R] must have naturally
begun in an environment with lowered uvula (it seems
to begin, in fact, in languages having nasalized
vowels) and been generalized to other environments.
Of course, the change may occur in a different manner,
namely through the borrowing of [R], but this is a
relexification, not a new rule. For while the development of [R] beside a nasalized vowel is natural
according to Principle 1b, the natural denasalization
of the vowel leaves [R] henceforth without a rationale.
But now it is merely a lexical entry, rather than the
result of some 'unnatural' rule in the language.

It has been seen that opposite changes can be
explained without abandoning Principle 1a by invoking
feature-reweighting, the special position, and crazy-
rule generalization, as well as other items involved
in Principle 1b (under which are included the implicational feature coefficients ⊃ and ⊂ discussed below,
which specify chain shifts; for others, see fn. 24).
Other ways for being true to data involving opposite
changes can be handled by distinguishing morphological
or morphophonic rules from phonological rules. Thus,
ablaut (though in pre-Indo-European doubtless a phonological relationship) is morphological in English, while
the vowel shift is phonological, and some metatheses are
morphological, while many are phonological. The phenomenon of rule-inversion (Vennemann MS) appears to be
amenable to this distinction. Another kind of opposite
changes or rules can of course be handled by the phenomenon of rule-inhibition, which is discussed elsewhere;

thus, an apparent unnatural change of $\underline{a}^e$ to $\underline{\vartheta}^i$ is due
to the inhibition of the natural change of $\underline{\vartheta}^i$ to $\underline{a}^e$.
Yet another variety of opposite changes involves the
change of an unglided vowel to a rising or falling
diphthongal nucleus and the converse. These phenomena
seem to be related to the interdependence of prosodic
phenomena discussed in fn. 24. Thus a shift in syl-
labication--due, e.g. to anaptyxis, vowel epenthesis,
syncope, or apocope--may result in a preference for a
different type of diphthong (rising or falling) or un-
diphthongized nucleus. A falling diphthong is unde-
sirable in a language that prefers unmarked syllabication (open syllables). Further, a rising diphthong
may become a pure vowel when the palatal or labio-
velar glide at its beginning is absorbed into the preceding consonant as a palatalization or rounding
feature.

Linguistic analyses using marking feature coefficients instead of static plusses and minuses have
directional change built into them. As for the natural
basis of unmarking and rule-generalization, it is to be
looked for in the acquisition of language by children.
Generalization is obvious: children perceive more
generally at first and only later with greater specif-
icity. Missing a feature makes a rule more general.
Assuming a correlation between markedness and relative
difficulty of acquiring, we may assume that when children fail to acquire a marked aspect of adult language,
perhaps because the language has (through borrowing by
adults or some other cause) exceeded the threshold of
their ability to acquire markings, they simply end up
with the unmarked equivalent.[36] Their failure to acquire a given mark results in a diachronic change of
marked to unmarked, which is only apparently paradox-
ical in the light of children's own acquisitional progress from unmarked to marked. It must be assumed that
children in some sense 'know' the directionality of
change, or at least of such changes as are 'natural',
i.e. due to the manner in which children acquire languages. The directionality of other changes,[37] due to
borrowing and hypercorrection must be assessed with the
help of relative quantities and Principle 20 (pg. 82).
It will be made clear later that the child must know
what classes prefer or shun a new phenomenon, i.e. what
the value of the social feature [favored] is for it.

For some changes, this awareness may be postponed
until the late teens.
    In view of the differing concepts of marking
and naturalness that abound today, it may be useful
to interpose here a few comments on the different
positions, all of which derive from Jakobson 1968
(first published 1941). Aside from the views of
Jakobsonians and Pragueans quite outside the generative tradition, those known to the writer either
share the generativist point of view of Chomsky &
Halle 1968 (e.g. Postal 1968, Schane 1968, and Cairns
1969, 1970) at one end of the spectrum or are asso-
ciated with a point of view not very different from
the 'natural phonology' proposed by David Stampe (cf.
Stampe MS). Nearer to the former pole, but distinct
from the point of view that prevails there, are the
views of Schachter 1969 and Vennemann 1972; nearer to
the other pole are Matthew Chen (see References) and
Schane 1972. All of these scholars employ plus and
minus values in phonological rules, although several
permit marking values in the lexicon. Those closer to
the outlook of generative phonology utilize marking
values to determine unique (non-arbitrary) underlying
representations of neutralized feature values, as a
metric or interpretative tool to adjudge the naturalness of rules, and to trigger what is known as <u>linking</u>
(Chomsky & Halle 419-35; see criticism in Bach & Harms
1972).
    Besides using ternary-valued features and marking
coefficients of features in phonological rules, the
position taken here differs from others chiefly in the
distinction between the two levels represented by
Principle 1a (feature-unmarking) and 1b (higher-level
natural rules) and in making use of the special position
in the syllable (cf. fn. 35) in differentiating the
making values of several features. Stampe, like the
generativists, makes no distinction between feature-
unmarking and natural rules, although he advocates only
the latter, while they maintain only the former. The
position taken here utilizes natural rules that both
unmark feature values--thus, marking theory is part of
the point of view maintained in this study--and perform
higher-level simplifications. This point of view has
been intimated by Vennemann 1972b:240, whose <u>typological
adjustment rules</u> have correspondences with the writer's

higher-level unmarking rules. (Vennemann's I-rules
show how different his position is, however; where
changes that increase markedness are not due to
borrowing, they can be handled as proposed in the
discussion of rules effecting opposite changes which
are discussed several paragraphs above.) Like other
scholars, the writer admits that the marking values
of lighter-weighted features may vary with different
values of heavier features, and that marking values
of features may differ according to the values of
features in adjacent segments (see the discussion of
[continuant] above and of [nuclear] in the Appendix).
But the present view differs from some in our not
having contex-sensitive non-markedness when due to
assimilation. Further, the writer's special position
goes a good deal beyond what has been accepted by
others (except Parker MS, where the present position
is anticipated, and--in a limited way--in Chen MSb)
and requires treating syllables as basic production
units. But it is the distinction between unmarking
feature values and higher-level natural rules which
is most important in enabling us to explain opposite
rules without abandoning (as in Miller 1972) the
principle of unidirectionality of natural changes.
Without this principle and the dynamic rules which
the use of marking values permit us to formulate, the
goal of polylectal grammars would be unthinkable.

3.1 Generation of subsystems. The advantages of
marking formulations in reconstructing underlying
representations for polylectal systems, whether 'synchronic' or 'diachronic', ought not to be overlooked.
A principle of internal reconstruction that follows
from Principle 1a in the preceding section is Principle 2a; Principle 2b has a similar logic:
  (2)   It is feasible to formulate a polylectal
        underlying representation to generate
        variants that differ
  (a)   in the value or relative weighting of a
        feature or in the ordering of a pair of
        rules, if the pre-unmarked feature value,
        weighting, or ordering is reconstructed;
        and
  (b)   in more and less general forms of rules,
        if the least general form of the rule--

     the one with the greatest number of feature
     constraints--is reconstructed.
The wording of Principle 2a mentions the 'pre-unmarked'
value of a feature instead of the 'marked' value in
order to take into account the 'unmarkings' specified
by Principle 1b as well as 1a. Principle 2a is valid
because what is unmarked can be generated--therefore
predicted and presumably more easily understood--from
what is marked. But the converse is not possible.[38]
Principle 2b depends on the fact that what is more
general can be generated from what is less general by
simply dropping a feature.[39] Principle 9 below purports
to specify that it is the heaviest-weighted variable
feature in a rule that gets deleted and the lightest
that gets reweighted when such generalizations and reweightings take place. Although what is more general
can be predicted from what is less general, it is the
more general formulation that implies the less general
one in tests like the one in Elliott et al. (Bailey
1973b).

  At this point it will be helpful to provide an
illustration of reweighting and its formulation in a
polylectal grammar. The example is based on data from
Labov 1969, 1972, and Labov, Cohen, Robins & Lewis 1968,
taken from samples of the speech of male Black speakers
in Harlem in New York City. It has to do with the patterns of deleting clustered word-final apical stops in
the presence or absence of two variables:

  (i) The presence or absence of an internal word
    boundary[40] between //t// and a preceding ob-
    struent and between //d// and a preceding //n//
    or lateral (in nonstandard speech, also an
    obstruent). (The boundary, which is present
    in miss#ed, bann#ed, bowl#ed, and bill#ed,
    is absent in mist, band, bold, and build.)
  (ii) The presence or absence of a vowel[41] at the
    beginning of the word that follows immediately,
    if in the same phonological phrase.

  The earlier form of the rule is given informally
as 3a below. Here the two variables have their marked
relative weights: [word boundary] is heavier than
[nuclear]. A reweighting to the opposite, unmarked
relative weighting yields rule 3b. The variable features in the rules are indicated by variable features
or by parentheses. (Rule 3a will be reformulated in

§3.3 as 3a'.)   Table 1 provides a calculus for the
four environments--a, b, c, and d of rule 3a according
to the principles outlined in the Appendix.   Table 2
does the same for environments a, b', c', and d of
rule 3b.   Note that in calculating environment weightings, minus weights give positive products when multiplied with minus feature coefficients, and negative
products when multiplied with plus feature values.   The
principles discussed in the next section provide that
rules operate 'faster' in heavier environments than in
lighter ones.[4,3]

(3a) $\left\{\begin{matrix} d \\ t \end{matrix}\right\}$ → ⍉ / C [-2 w.b.] __ ## [-1 nuc]

(3b) $\left\{\begin{matrix} d \\ t \end{matrix}\right\}$ → ⍉ / C [-1 w.b.] __ ## [-2 nuc]

Table 1.   Calculus for rule 3a in the temporally successive
environments, a, b, c, and d.

		[-2 w.b.]	[-1 nuc]	Total
Env. a	mist ## [- nuc]	-2 X - = +2	-1 X - = +1	+3
Env. b	mist ## [+ nuc]	-2 X - = +2	-1 X + = -1	+1
Env. c	miss#ed ## [- nuc]	-2 X + = -2	-1 X - = +1	-1
Env. d	miss#ed ## [+ nuc]	-2 X + = -2	-1 X + = -1	-3

Table 2.   Calculus for rule 3b in the temporally successive
environments, a, b', c', and d.

		[-1 w.b.]	[-2 nuc]	Total
Env. a	mist ## [- nuc]	-1 X - = +1	-2 X - = +2	+3
Env. b'	miss#ed ## [- nuc]	-1 X + = -1	-2 X - = +2	+1
Env. c'	mist ## [+ nuc]	-1 X - = +1	-2 X + = -2	-1
Env. d	miss#ed ## [+ nuc]	-1 X + = -1	-2 X + = -2	-3

Deletion in the heaviest environment is of course
normal in both American and British standard pronunciation. (See fn. 41.) Most of the male Blacks investigated by Labov and his associates had rule 3b in casual
conversation. But in the style used with an inter-
viewer present, working-class teenagers and adults who
had lived mostly in the North had rule 3a. Pre-
adolescent boys, as well as adults who had lived in
the South in their early years, used rule 3b in the
interview style. Isolated pre-adolescents who did not
belong to gangs (the lames) and middle-class adult
Black males used 3a in the interview style. Thus, the
newer (reweighted) form of rule 3 is characteristic of
youthfulness and informality or lower educational status

The comments in the preceding paragraph about the
relative recentness of rule 3b assume normal linguistic
change. But it is likely that the actual directionality of time is just the reverse for many speakers.
This is because the process of decreolizing an original
Black Creole involves changes of unmarked to marked by
borrowing English marked phenomena in place of creole
unmarked phenomena. Since the criteria for directionality of change are reversed in such cases, the result
is the same: 3b has the unmarked weightings of the
variable features found in rules 3a and 3b. That we
may be dealing with natural changes here, rather than
decreolization, may possibly be deduced from the fact
that the standard English rule (operative rarely in all
but the earliest environment) is the 'later' 3b, not
the 'earlier' 3a.

Let us now turn to marked and unmarked rule orderings, a subject for which the literature representing
new points of view is becoming copious. New views are
being represented by Anderson 1969, Kiparsky 1971, and
King MS. Koutsoudas, Sanders & Noll MS, Koutsoudas MSa
and MSb, Ringen MS, Norman 1972, and Lehmann 1972, as
well as Vennemann 1972, claim that there is no extrinsic rule ordering, i.e. that universally valid principles uniquely determine the applicational priority
of any two rules, if they have any ordering relationship to each other[43] The following discussion will
show that this assumption is not tenable. Nevertheless, the general principles advocated by Koutsoudas
et al. and by Vennemann may well define unmarked rule
order, the order to which a marked ordering may give

way in the natural development of a language system.
At all events, the result of the work referred to in
this paragraph is to take linguistic theory much
closer to a position in which no two rules can have
both their relative orderings marked or unmarked, but
where one ordering will be uniquely unmarked and the
other marked.

The examples of reordering which follow are both
amenable to the principle of maximizing feeding order
first proposed in Kiparsky 1968. (Many more examples
are found in Bailey 1973c.) Both of the examples to
follow probably began (variably) in allegro pronunciations, when monitoring was minimal and the suppression
of unmarking ceased to prevail (cf. fn. 36). The first
example is an example of a lexical exception to the
prevailing rule order of a single lect, according to
principles proposed in Bailey 1968b and later established in Anderson 1969. Both examples show how different lects of the same overall system are differentiated by ordering differences[44]

1. Rules iii and iv are required for all (non-
creolized) varieties of 'r-less' English and are relevant to the intermediate representation of <u>pattern</u>,
/'pætɚn/. In the order shown below, iii-iv, they
convert this representation to /'pætən/, which is
changed by later rules to become the phonetic output
of Southern States English: ['phædən]. Since rule iii
cannot operate on the representation /'pætɚn/ if not
preceded by rule iv, this is the marked order. (Rule
iv generates [n̩] in <u>Patton</u> and <u>paten</u>.)

(iii) Unaccented /ən/ becomes [n̩] following non-
syllable-initial (unclustered and non-word
initial) /d t ð b/ and following /z s/
(also /ž š/ in BRP and in fast tempos of
other lects), whether syllable-initial or
not.

(iv) The sulcal vowel /ɚ/ (which is found as a
syllabic peak only in unaccented syllables)
is changed to /ə/ (i.e. it is desulcalized)[45]

But in New England and in the so-called 'received pronunciation' of England, the rules just given have their
unmarked ordering, iv-iii, in which both rules operate
on the form /'pætɚn/. Rule iv first changes this to
/pætən/, which is then changed to /pætn̩/ by rule iii,
resulting in a merger of the output of <u>pattern</u> with the
output of <u>Patton</u>.

But even Southern States English, with its marked
order, iii-iv, has exceptions like <u>modern</u> ['mᵊdn̦],
generated with the unmarked order, iv-iii. Since this
variety of English would have the marked order, iii-iv,
as the normal order of its grammar, some notation for
exceptional lexical items must indicate that rule iv
has its unmarked order. It is important to note that
this order can be predicted from the marked order. For
this reason, the panlectal grammar of English would
adopt the marked ordering. Lects having the unmarked
ordering for all lexical items on which the rules could
operate are simply marked in the grammar and in speakers' minds for an across-the-board reordering.
　　2. The next example to be considered involves
rules v and vi, given here in their marked order:

(v)　A lateral not followed by a vowel is changed
　　　to become the satellite of a preceding
　　　nucleus.[46] (The satellite is written[ˡ:];
　　　note the length indicator.)

(vi)　Unaccented /ü/ (generated from underlying
　　　//u// standing before a weak consonantal
　　　cluster followed by an underlying vowel)
　　　is changed to /yə/.

The operation of these rules (in the order shown) can
be illustrated with Southern States <u>volume</u> ['vᵊlyəm
'vᵊyem -əm], <u>value</u> ['vælyə 'væyə -ə], and <u>valiant</u>
['vælyə̃t 'væyə̃t].[47] from underlying //vn̦lume　vālue
vāl+iant//.[48] Rule v cannot operate on these forms unless rule vi has previously created a consonant (viz.
/y/) immediately after the //l//. This later, unmarked
ordering, in which both rules vi and v operate in turn
on the underlying representations of these examples is
what in fact generates the Northern States pronunciations: ['vɑˡ:yem -əm 'væˡ:yə -ə 'væˡ:yə̃t].
　　The variants just discussed in both of the preceding examples do not differ in their underlying representations, but only in the rule orderings of the lects
in question.[49]
　　It is being taken for granted here that rules are
added at the end of the rule component[50] to which they
belong (cf. King MS), although simultaneous reordering
to an unmarked position higher up is possible. And the
writer accepts the view (discussed, e.g. in Anderson
1969) that rules are normally applied in iterative
fashion. This is clearly the case with PIE [syllabic],

in harmony languages (like Turkish, where an anharmonic segment interrupts the process), and in generating intonational patterns in English (Bailey MS).

Mention has been made (fn. 36) of unmarking processes which operate in adult speech because of haste, fatigue, or emotional upset, conditions that reduce self-monitoring[61] Conversely, late rules which unmark even normal informal styles are suspended in more monitored, formal, or over-correct styles; cf. the study of 'Sunday Greek' by Kazazis (1968). The obvious reason for this is that late rules make phonetic outputs more unlike underlying representations (including, for literates, the spelling) than they would be without such late rules. The most monitored pronunciation is employed for disambiguating. If the late rule that changes syllable-final /t/ to [d] intervocalically is suspended, [t] will be heard in mettle and metal (cf. metalic), which are distinct from medal (cf. medallion) and meddle. If 'r-less' speakers suspend their late rule iv (see above), spar (cf. sparring) will be kept distinct from spa.

Rule-inhibition has been misinterpreted by variationists and also by other authorities on rule ordering. To justify the sulcalization of /ə/ or the change of /a^e a^o/ to /ə^i e^u/ would require such an extreme view of rule-inversion that the justification of natural-language rules in terms of historically valid changes would be impossible. Note that Kiparsky 1968, which specifically accepts this principle (and it has not been overthrown in Bach and Harms 1972, once the hierarchy of markings is understood; cf. fn. 24), quite correctly speaks of 'the loss of word-final devoicing in Swiss German and Yiddish' (1968:190). Other generative phonologists have not always been so careful.

If we assume that unmarked rule ordering is simply the absence of ordering (fn. 43), so that an unordered rule may operate repeatedly as an 'anywhere rule', then unmarking the order of a rule will unmark any marked-order relation it has with every other rule, not simply the marked relation between it and one or some of the other rules. This interesting assumption appears to have been corroborated in a rather complex example from Carden's (1970) thesis, which will now be discussed. In his thesis, Carden discovered four isolects differing with respect to the orderings of three rules:

TAG (<u>Tag-Question Formation</u>), QL (<u>Quantifier-Lowering</u>),
and NT (<u>Not-Transportation</u>). The lects which Carden
had discovered in 1970 were W, X, Y, and Z in Fig. 1;

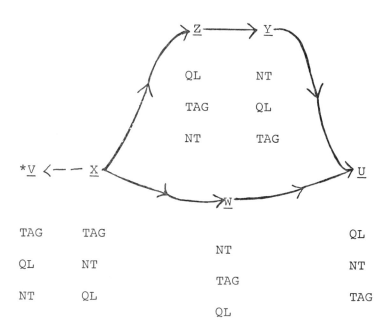

Fig. 1. Succession of Lects Generated from Lect X
         by Successive Reorderings of a Single Rule
         to its Maximally Unmarked Order with Respect
         to Each of the Other Rules. (Arrow heads
         indicate the directionality of the changes;
         broken shaft of the arrow pointing to the
         impossible lect, V, indicates a reordering
         forbidden by the theory.)

X has all the rules in their mutually marked orderings,
orderings from which all the other mathematically possible lects could be derived. Carden predicted that
isolects represented by the other two orderings, shown
in Fig. 1 as U and V, would also be possible. And he
in fact later went looking for them. Bailey 1970
questioned the possibility of lect V, while granting
that U, where all the rule orderings are unmarked, would
indeed be possible. The reason for ruling out lect V
was that it could be generated from X only through a
partial reordering, i.e. a reordering of a rule with

respect to only one of the other rules. Subsequent
investigations by Carden have provided a large number
of instances of U, but none of V.

Despite the impressive apparent corroboration of
the view that rules cannot unmark partially, but only
in toto, further research (Bailey 1973c:237) suggests
that it may require modification. Obviously, further
checking is in order.

The writer has for several years been of the
opinion that rule-deletion comes about through changes
to unmarked order. In Bailey 1973a, it was pointed
out that, if the marked order of rules (a) $y \rightarrow z$ and
(b) $x \rightarrow y$ is unmarked to permit (b) to feed (a), so
that $x \rightarrow y \rightarrow z$, a restructuring would occur: Rule (b)
would be dropped, and the input to (a) would be gen-
eralized as both x and y--or only x, if x should become the sole source of y, in which event y would be
eliminated from lexical representations. Such changes
would not take place in a polylectal grammar until
practically all its subsystems had undergone the reordering in question. Lack of space prevents extended
discussion of rule-deletion, which can perhaps be caused
by creolization also, but the foregoing will suggest
what may be involved.

All such changes take effect gradually, and no
doubt items which are eliminated from the language disappear in some implicational sequence[52] A possible
explanation for chain shifts (like the consonant shifts
in Armenian and German or the chain palatalizations in
Slavic and French, for some discussion of which cf.
Dressler 1971) which utilizes an aspect of marking
theory was put forward several years ago in Greenberg
1966:95-6. (See also Lass 1971.) While it may be that
changes which destroy the expected implicational relationships among items in the inventory of a language
demand the restoration of the proper relationship,
either by changing the implicans to the implicate or by
restoring the implicate in some manner, there are enough
problems connected with this view to be cautious about
it. However, the reasonableness of this theory warrants
a fair testing for it[53] Changes that result in some
sort of additional markedness of an environment or
lower-level feature can be tolerated until the language
gets too marked for children to be able to acquire it.
Once their threhold is exceeded, they will fail to acquire some marks of their native language.

Earlier and later changes and environments of
changes can be built into rule formulations with implicational feature coefficients. These are illustrated
below with rules of my own proposing and three rules
from Chen MSb, where a quite different notation is
found. (The notation [! lower] is proposed in Miller
1972:140 to denote "the increasing likelihood" of a
rule's operation with respect to a lower vowel.) In
the notation proposed here, $\lceil \supset F_i \rceil$ indicates that the
plus value of a feature is relevant to the rule before
the mid value ($[x\ F_i]$), and that the mid value is
relevant prior to the minus value. This temporal se-
quencing of $[+\ F_i]$ before $\lceil x\ F_i \rceil$ before $\lceil -\ F_i \rceil$ <u>creates</u>
the overall implicational patterning in the language,
$[-\ F_i] \supset [x\ F_i] \supset [+\ F_i]$. When the value of a feature
is $[\subset]$, its minus value is prior to its mid, and that
is prior to its plus value. Where an input $[\supset F_i]$ or
$[\subset F_i]$ effects a chain shift, one step of which changes
an input $\lceil u\ low \rceil$ ($[+\ low]$) vowel to an output $[M\ low]$
($[x\ low]$, or mid) vowel, as in rule 11 below, we see
Principle 1b overruling Principle 1a. The same is true
of the assimilatory rule 5a below, which changes unmarked values of input features to marked values in the
outputs. Of course, an input unmarked feature does not
violate Principle 1a if some other feature is the one
that is changed in the output, as in rules 4a and 6a.
Thus, rule 4a stipulates that like changes affect
$[-\ grave]$, or front, vowels prior to affecting $[x\ grave]$
(mid-grave or central) vowels; and these before
$[+grave]$, or back, vowels.

The illustrative rules that follow show how dynamic formulations are possible and how they permit
the linguist to break out of the straitjacket of the
static framework.[54] Rules 5a, 5b, and 6a are assimilatory. Since 6b merely reverses 6a, both are combined in rule 7.

(4a) $\begin{bmatrix} V \\ \subset \text{grave} \end{bmatrix} \rightarrow \dots$

(4b) $\begin{matrix} \text{C} \\ \supset \text{voiced} \end{matrix} \rightarrow \dots$

(5) $\begin{bmatrix} \text{C} \\ \supset \text{lingual} \end{bmatrix} \rightarrow \left\{ \begin{matrix} \text{(a)} \begin{bmatrix} \text{u grave} \\ \text{M lingual} \\ \text{m dorsal} \end{bmatrix} / \underline{\quad} \begin{bmatrix} \text{u nuclear} \\ \text{u grave} \\ \subset \text{low} \end{bmatrix} \\ \\ \text{(b)} \begin{bmatrix} \text{M continuant} \\ \text{m voiced} \end{bmatrix} / \text{V} \underline{\quad} \text{V} \end{matrix} \right\}$

(6a) $\begin{bmatrix} V \\ \subset \text{grave} \\ \supset \text{low} \end{bmatrix} \rightarrow [\text{m nasal}] / \underline{\quad} [\text{u nasal}]$

(6b) $\begin{bmatrix} V \\ \supset \text{grave} \\ \subset \text{low} \end{bmatrix} \rightarrow [\text{u nasal}] / \underline{\quad} [\text{m nasal}]$

(7) $\begin{bmatrix} V \\ \alpha \subset \text{grave} \\ \alpha \supset \text{low} \end{bmatrix} \rightarrow [\text{n nasal}] / \underline{\quad} [\alpha \text{ u nasal}]$

where $-\supset = \subset$, where $-\subset = \supset$, where $-\underline{u} = \underline{m}$ or $\underline{M}$, and
where $\underline{n}$ abbreviates $\underline{u}$ in non-assimilatory natural
rules, but an assimilatory value (here: plus)
in assimilatory rules (cf. Schachter 1969)[55]

Rules 4a, b are really metarules governing other,
substantive rules; e.g. 5a, b should include the input
feature [$\supset$ voiced].

Rule 5 changes consonantal inputs in this sequence:
first [+ lingual] consonants, or dorsals (in 5a: velars);
then [x lingual] consonants, or apicals; and finally,
[- lingual] consonants, or labials.   The change generated by 5b is lenition, i.e. the change of intervocalic
obstruents to voiced continuants.   The output feature
[M continuant] denotes a fricative only if the segment
in question is prenuclear.   If it should turn out
to be true that such assimilations occur also in syllable-final intervocalic obstruents (as appears to be
the case with the rule illustrated in American English
beater ['bidɚ]), the rule will have to be complicated
accordingly, but this is not necessary for the present
illustration.

Rule 5a palatalizes inputs before front vowels--
first, if these front vowels are [- low], i.e. high;
next, if they are [x low], i.e. mid; and lastly, if
they are [+ low]. For the intersequencing of the nine
outputs resulting from the interaction of the two
variables in rule 5a, see §3.3.

Rule 6a generates a nasalized vowel before a segment that is unmarked for the feature [nasal]--which
in the special position can only be a nasal consonant.
The rule stipulates that the change occurs in [+ low]
vowels before occurring in [x low] vowels; and that
[- low] vowels are the last (and least likely) ones to
be affected by the rule. Note also that grave inputs
are affected before non-grave inputs, which are less
likely to undergo rule 6a. With rule 6b, which de-
nasalizes vowels, everything is reversed. Consequently,
6a and 6b are combined as rule 7. Note that rule 6a
agrees with 4a while 6b--if indeed it should mention
[⊃ grave] in the input--merely reverses the assimilation of 6a.

Many more natural rules remain to be written.
There will be rules specifying the raising of long and
close vowels and one specifying the lowering of short
and open vowels (but cf. fnn. 60, 73, where certain
problems connected with 'tense' and 'lax' vowels are
discussed). As already observed, rule 4a should be
superimposed on rules 5a and 5b in the manner that
rule 4b already has been on 6a in the above formulation.
Another rule will provide that vowel-raising changes
usually begin in oxytonic syllables before [⊂ grave]
consonants, while another will provide that vowel-
lowering rules operate first in paroxytonic environments before word boundaries and subsequently before
[⊂ lingual] consonants (cf. §4.2), eventually spreading from paroxytonic to oxytonic syllables. The facts
surrounding the diphthongization of //ī// (cf. fn. 73)
show that rhythmic and incremental length have opposite
effects on the rate of that change. This rule operates
earlier in paroxytonic vowels, where rhythmic shortening occurs, but later in vowels followed by heavy
(underlying voiceless) obstruents, where the vowel is
shorter than in environments followed by light (underlying voiced) consonants. Some linguistic evidence
indicates that /ö/ unrounds prior to the unrounding of
/ü/; here the input is [⊃ low].

In the Western states speakers lose underlying
//x// (which changes a preceding //ɒ// to /ɔ/, no less than
do other heavy fricatives in other varieties of English,
as in cost, soft, and cloth) in the environment
[⊂ lingual]. The loss occurs earlier in dauber than
in naughty, caught, and dawn (see fn. 73), and reaches
hawk last. The result is to make dauber rhyme with
robber and the other words to sound like knotty, cot
don, and hock, respectively. The reason why the operation of the rule specifying the change in question in
a more recent environment implicates its operation in
an earlier one is explained in §4.1 below. The rule
strengthening the heavy consonants in High German affects input [⊂ grave, ⊂ lng] ones, where [grave] is
the heavier feature: the only [- grave] heavy consonant is t, and it is affected first; of [x grave]
inputs, p is affected prior to k. (I ignore the special
cases where the inputs are adjacent to liquids.) In
these instances (as in chain shifts), M, m, and u coefficients do not suffice; for one thing, the order of
the consonants is probably the same both in prenuclear
and postnuclear parts of the syllable.
    For fully natural rules, there is required a prin-
ciple, not yet formulated, which specifies which feature pairs can be linked with Greek-letter variables
(for a discussion of other principles relating to these,
cf. Principles 9c and 10 below).
    Rule-inversion (Vennemann MS) has already been
discussed. (The kind of rule-reversal found in decreolization as the result of borrowing of course
poses no problems for the matter under discussion.)
It may be worth pointing out here that even if some
or all of the models already discussed and the principles and models to follow should prove grossly inadequate, the present proposals are not without value,
since they show how a dynamic analysis could work, and
since they therefore show that a dynamic grammar is
quite feasible.

3.2 Exposition of metalinguistic principles. It is
being taken for granted that Labov 1966 and 1969,
together with other work still unpublished, has made
unassailable all but the (a) part of Principle 8.
    (8) New rules are added at the end of their
         component of the grammar, and they begin

               (a) in a very limited environment,
               (b) variably--in this first and in
               each successive environment--and (c)
               often with a feature or two in a marked
               relative weighting.
(See some discussion on the gradualness of change in
Schourup 1972.) Much work remains to be done in order
to ascertain the conditions operating on rules at their
inception. But the provisional principles below--9 is
very tentative--will show what features are altered and
how, as the rule spreads beyond its original, limited
environment. The sequencing of the operations defined
in Principles 9 and 10 are discussed in §3.3. Principle 10 will be augmented with Principle 19 in the
discussion of the wave model in §4.1.

(9a)   When natural developments delete a rule
feature--i.e. generalize its value to a
Greek-letter variable ranging over all
feature values used in the system--to
make the rule more general: heavier-
weighted variable features in a given
part of the rule (either input or environment) are changed earlier than lighter
variable features in that part of the rule.[56]

(9b)   When a feature is reweighted to its unmarked relative weighting: lighter-weighted
variable features are affected earlier than
heavier ones in the same part of the rule.[57]

(9c)   When values of implicational feature coefficients $(\subset, \supset)$ are changed: lighter-
weighted variable features are affected
earlier than heavier-weighted ones.

(10)   Since heavier environments are earlier and
faster than lighter ones, it may be said
that rules effect changes at a faster rate,
i.e. earlier, in greater quantity, and to a
greater extent, in the presence of (a)
heavier-weighted variable features;[58] a
faster rate also accompanies (b) a marked
value, if the coefficient is a Greek-letter
variable; and (c) a plus value if the coefficient is $\supset$, and a minus value if it is
$\subset$. (Note that 10b pertains only to variable
features, sometimes parenthesized in variable
rules.)

It seems probable too that we should regard higher
items in curly brackets as faster or earlier than lower
ones. Note the Greek-letter variable, ω, first suggested by Chin-Wu Kim to represent the extreme values
of a multivalued feature, i.e. plus and minus in a
ternary system. Note that [α F] may refer to the
absolute (plus, mid, or minus) values of [ω F] or to
the marking values of [α F] or [ᾱ F] (where the bar
above negates the value). Principle 10 ensures that
when [α F_i] and [α F_j] or [ᾱ F_j] appear in the same
segment (where $F_i > F_j$), the [m F_i, u F_j] values will
have a faster rate than [u F_i, m F_j]. Principle 10c
is an example of a higher-level (viz. chain-shift) unmarking which overrules feature-unmarking according to
Principle 1b, as already noted.

Before illustrating the application of these principles, it should be pointed out that there are two
ways in which they can combine to cause the acceleration of an originally slower input or environment
variable ahead of an originally faster one. Principle
9b may combine with 10a, or Principle 9a may combine
with 10b. To take the latter case first, if an input
feature is generalized (according to Principle 9a) from
[u F_i] to [ɑ F_i], then Principle 10b dictates that
[m F_i] will--after an interim of readjustment perhaps--
be faster than [u F_i], even though the rule operated
with [u F_i] before the generalization to include [m F_i].
See the input to rule 11 below for an example. Similarly, if a lighter-weighted and slower variable environment feature is, in line with Principle 9b, reweighted to a heavier weight, Principle 10a will cause
the environment of the reweighted variable feature to
become faster than those it had been reweighted over,
even though they were faster before the reweighting.
This will also be illustrated in rule 11. Note that
the principles just enunciated make empirically vul-
nerable predictions. For example, there should be no
acceleration of the first sort, i.e. due to reweighting,
in rules where features have their unmarked relative
weightings.

The example to be given now is based on Labov
1972a[59]. Labov points out that /æ/ is 'tensed' (i.e.
changed from the unmarked [x pharyngeal widening] to
the marked [+ pharyngeal widening])[60] before (a)
heavy (i.e. underlying voiceless) fricatives,

abbreviated F; (b) light (i.e. underlying voiced)
stops, which are abbreviated \$; and (c) nasals, abbre-
viated N. The resulting 'tense' vowel is written /ǣ/.
As a result of this prior rule, the F and \$ environ-
ments can be unambiguously designated as [α continuant,
β voiced], provided they are non-nasal. Features in
rule 11 that lack implicational coefficients or parentheses are categorical, i.e. non-variable parts of the
rule. Within a given segment, heavier-weighted features are written above lighter ones.

$$(11) \quad \begin{bmatrix} V \\ m\ accent \\ (u\ grave) \\ \supset low \\ m\ phar.\ wid. \end{bmatrix} \rightarrow [\supset low] / \underline{\quad} \begin{bmatrix} (m\ continuant) \\ (u\ voiced) \\ \subset nasal \end{bmatrix} C_0 \#$$

Table 3.   Isolects generated by rule 11.

| | | | Stage i | | | | | | Stage ii | |
| | | | Isolect | | | | | | Isolect | |
1	2	3	4	5	6	7	8	9	10	11
(F)	(F)	(F)	(\$)	(N)	N	N	(N)	(N)	N	N
	(\$)	(\$)	(F)	(\$)	(\$)	\$		(\$)	(\$)	\$
		(N)	(N)	(F)	(F)	F		(F)	(F)	F

Earlier lects, or earlier environments for the operation
of rule 11 in a given lect, are to the left; later ones
are on the right. Stage i represents the change of a
low nucleus to a mid one; stage ii represents the change
from mid to high.

Rule 11 changes a [+ phar. wid.] (tense) low (later
mid also) nucleus to a mid (later high also) nucleus in
a word-final accented syllable before F, \$, and N at
rates specified by Principles 9 and 10. (The use of
the feature [pharyngeal widening in this rule is problematic, in view of the designation of underlying and post
vowel-change heavy vowels the same way. But see fn. 73;
it is possible that [peripheral] could be used here.)
Isolect 1 represents the (long since past) fastest environment in operation--[m cnt, u voi, m nas], i.e. F.
If the heaviest variable feature (viz. [(m cnt)])

generalizes first according to Principle 9a, it cannot represent either of the other two possible environments ($ or N) without further changes in other
features[61] so no new isolect can result. But when
[u voi] is then generalized to include the specification [m voi], both $ and F environments are now
specified, viz. as [α cnt,β voi, m nas]. The result
is the unattested isolect 2. Then Principle 10b
dictates that $ ([M cnt, m voi, m nas]) should ac-
celerate ahead of F after a period of readjustment,
during which the change might occur in the two environments at equal rates. The data from Labov show
that the lightest-weighted variable feature in the
environment ([$\supset$ nas]) generalizes during this interim,
creating isolect 3 (attested in Labov 1972a:137). The
reweighting of $ and F is consummated in isolect 4,
which is not attested.

Isolect 5 is attested in the speech of a sixty-
year-old Jewish male (Labov 1972a:144). It is notable
that in the speech of this informant the input has
generalized, according to Principle 9a, to [α grave]
so that rule 11 affects back-vowel as well as front-
vowel inputs. Indeed, the change effected by rule 11
is more advanced for back vowels in the speech of the
informant for isolect 5 than for front vowels, as
stipulated in Principle 10b. The informant in ques-
tion has raised /$\bar{\mathrm{o}}$/ to a position as high as, or higher
than, /$\bar{\mathrm{æ}}$/ has reached in any environment in his speech.
The ordering of the successive generalizations and reweightings in rule 11 will be discussed in §3.3. The
form which rule 11 has in isolect 5 is shown as rule 12:

$$(12) \quad \begin{bmatrix} V \\ m \text{ accent} \\ \gamma \text{ grave} \\ u \text{ low} \\ u \text{ phar. wid.} \end{bmatrix} \rightarrow [M \text{ low}] \;/\; \underline{\quad} \; \left\{ \begin{array}{c} [u \text{ nas.}] \\ \begin{bmatrix} \alpha \text{ cont} \\ \beta \text{ voi} \\ m \text{ nas} \end{bmatrix} \end{array} \right\} C_o \;\#\#$$

Once generalizations and reweightings have brought
about changes in the rate of inputs and environments
in rule 11, these remain until further changes that
accord with Principles 9 and 10 take place; the originally earliest environment will not be earliest in
the second stage of rule 11. But before discussing
stage ii, it is necessary to conclude our consideration

of stage i. Labov refers to isolect 6, but gives no
example of it. He refers to isolect 7 as exemplified
in earlier documentation.

Stage ii is represented by the second stage of
the output, viz. the change from a mid to a high
position. The output for this rule (as for other
examples) then goes through an isolectal series that
parallels the isolects of stage i, except that the
relative rates of the three environments is now per-
manently reweighted. Isolect 8 is represented by a
Jewish male aged 57 (Labov 1972a:146), who, incidentally, lacks the acceleration of the back-vowel
input. Isolect 9 is represented by a twenty-three-
year-old Jewish male (Labov 1972a:148). His speech
shows the acceleration of input/ɔ̄/ ahead of /ǣ/.
Labov speaks as though some females have reached
isolect 10, but 11 can only be found in very informal
styles, if at all, in New York City.

The rule that tenses /æ/ has been generalized
to all preconsonantal environments in Buffalo, where
rule 11 now variably generates stage ii outputs in
all of them. In other words, the last part of rule 11
is to be parenthesized as an environment variable,
the lightest-weighted of all: $(C_0\#\#)_4$. This advanced
development suggests the possibility that Buffalo
might be the origin of the rules. Detroit and Des
Plains (a suburb of Chicago) have the rule that
tenses /æ/ generalized to all preconsonantal environments. Labov thinks that the reweighting which made N
the fastest preconsonantal environment had already
occurred when rule 11 began in Detroit. Detroit has
isolect 8 already attested, but Des Plaines may not
have developed beyond stage i. It is evident that,
as rule 11 spread to the West, changes in the environment outpaced the extension of the output to stage ii,
in contrast with what happened in the East.

3.3 Interrelations of time factors in rules. We have
seen several instances of rules having temporal sequencings in more than one part of the same rule--input,
environment, and output--as in rules 5 and 11. This
raises the question of how the temporal sequencings are
meshed together in the single dimension of real time.
It has already been observed that most of the rules of
the sort being considered show the progression of a

given output through all the sequences defined by the
variables in the structural description (i.e. input
and environment). This may be called the normal situation; it does not always obtain. It has also been
noted in connection with the developments of rule 11
in Detroit and New York City that the changes in the
environment did not precede stage i in the latter, but
did precede stage i in Detroit. Here is a difference
in the intersequencing of the temporal changes in the
output and in the environment. Further, it has been
pointed out that isolect 8 in New York does not have
the input feature [(u grave)] generalized to [α grave],
although this generalization has occurred in isolects
7 and 9. Here is illustrated a difference in the intersequencing of the inputs and outputs of rule 11.

    The problem may be made clearer by showing the
different sequences of the nine outputs of rule 5a according to whether the input feature [lingual] is
heavier or lighter than the environment feature [low].
When input [lingual] is heavier than output [low], the
outputs are sequenced from earlier to later as follows:

$$
\begin{array}{ll}
\text{Dorsals} \ / \ \underline{\quad} & i \\
\text{Dorsals} \ / \ \underline{\quad} & e \\
\text{Dorsals} \ / \ \underline{\quad} & a \\
\text{Apicals} \ / \ \underline{\quad} & i \\
\text{Apicals} \ / \ \underline{\quad} & e \\
\text{Apicals} \ / \ \underline{\quad} & a \\
\text{Labials} \ / \ \underline{\quad} & i \\
\text{Labials} \ / \ \underline{\quad} & e \\
\text{Labials} \ / \ \underline{\quad} & a \\
\end{array}
$$

(Cf. the discussion of Tables 1 and 2 in §3.1.)   If
the input feature [lingual] is lighter-weighted than
the environment feature [low], the sequencing of the
outputs from earlier to later is as follows:

$$
\begin{array}{ll}
\text{Dorsals} \ / \ \underline{\quad} & i \\
\text{Apicals} \ / \ \underline{\quad} & i \\
\text{Labials} \ / \ \underline{\quad} & i \\
\text{Dorsals} \ / \ \underline{\quad} & e \\
\text{Apicals} \ / \ \underline{\quad} & e \\
\text{Labials} \ / \ \underline{\quad} & e \\
\text{Dorsals} \ / \ \underline{\quad} & a \\
\text{Dorsals} \ / \ \underline{\quad} & a \\
\text{Dorsals} \ / \ \underline{\quad} & a \\
\end{array}
$$

Perhaps general principles will be discovered to
show which of the above is more natural. Of course,
the explanation may well lie simply in feature weightings. But it may lie in universal principles which
dictate what the unmarked temporal priorities are among
input, environment, and output. If the explanation
lies in feature weightings, then numerical weights (as
in rule 3 above) would be the most natural notation to
suggest itself. But if the explanation lies in more
general principles governing the sequencing of different parts of a rule, then the more natural notation
might be rate indexes, attached as conditions to rules
or (in the case of a monolectal rule) written over the
arrow. Such rate indexes might simply abbreviate
generalizations and reweightings in the environment as
G and R, respectively, and those in the input as g and
r; successive outputs or stages in the change represented by the rule could be designated with subscript
i, ii, etc. Principles 9 and 10 would define which
features were to be affected by G, R, g, and r. The
code symbols could be sequenced from left to right in
the order of time above the arrow in a rule. The change
discussed in the preceding section developed differently in its westward spread from the way it developed
in New York City. In New York City, the sequence of
developments presumably (not all the facts are known
about the [+ grave] input) has been: two environmental
reweightings and then generalization of input [grave],
both of which occurred before stage ii was completed;
the deletion of the part of the environment specifying
oxytonesis has barely begun. Thus the rate index might
be: $[RR]_i[g(G)]_{ii}$. The deletion of the segmental environment has not yet begun in New York City, as in
Buffalo and the locales to the west. (Note that the
change in question moves from city to city, usually
skipping over the countryside.) In the Midwest, both
the segmental environment and the part of the environment specifying oxytonesis have been deleted from the
rule, but stage ii (output ii) has not been reached,
at least in some areas, nor has input [+ grave] yet
become involved. Here the rate indices are:
$[RRGG]_i([g]_{ii})$. If, as seems probable, this is the
unmarked weighting of the rate indices and the New York
City sequence represents their marked weighting, then
the indices tend toward an unmarked situation in which

environmental changes (feature-reweightings and generalizations) are prior to input generalizations.
It should be noted here that in most of the analyses
of changes in process examined, environmental changes
occur in order during each (output) stage of a rule
change. This in fact appears to be the normal algorithm for rate indices.

   If rule 3a is slightly rewritten as 3a', the
intersequencing of the outputs of the rule is provided for by both the implicational coefficients and
the weighting operators:

(3a') $\left\{ \begin{matrix} \underline{d} \\ \underline{t} \end{matrix} \right\}$ → ∅ / C [2⊂ w.b.] __ ## [1⊂ nuc]

(See Fasold 1970 for the use of numerical weighting
operators.) The initial environment is (a) [u w.b.,
u nuc]. When the implicational value of the lighter
feature changes, as provided by Principle 9c, it becomes [m nuc], since [M nuc] (the satellite of a
compound nucleus) is not possible here. When the
value of the heavier-weighted feature changes to
[M w.b.], we have the situation in pas+t, which is
more like the environment in mist (containing no
boundary) but actually promoting the rule's operation
more than in mist but less than in pass#ed or miss#ed.
As the heavier feature becomes [m w.b.], the environment is (c) [m w.b., u nuc], as when pass#ed and
miss#ed are followed by a non-vowel. Note that the
lighter-weighted feature has reverted to its original
u value. In fact, Principle 13 governs the intersequencing of such weighted features:
   (13) When a heavier-weighted variable feature
        changes its value, the successively
        lightest-weighted variable features that
        have implicational coefficients go through
        the entire sequence of values provided in
        Principles 10b and 10c.
A heavier-weighted variable feature would not, of
course, be reweighted before a lighter variable feature (Principle 9c). An examination of the sequencing
of environment relative weightings in Table 1 will
show why Principles 9b and 13 have to be as stated.
Only in this way will lighter-weighted features actually have less effects on variable rules, i.e. in the

calculus of the environments[6.2]   The last environment
in which rule 3a' operates is (d) [m w.b., m nuc].

One who believes in the universality of natural
developments in language will entertain a sanguine
view of the possibility of simplifying rules like 11
because of future insights on the general conditions
governing the initial forms of new rules.

4 THE WAVE MODEL, LANGUAGE COMMUNITIES AND SPEECH COMMUNITIES

4.0 <u>The language community</u>. The framework which is
assumed for the present undertaking is one in which
the notion of 'the [English] language' is taken quite
seriously. Those who communicate competently in
English, with all its variants, are assumed to constitute the <u>language community</u> of English-users.
The resources of English, and in particular its patterns of variation, may be allocated in different
ways within different <u>speech communities</u>[63] e.g.
'r-lessness' is highly valued and 'r-fulness' lowly
valued in some speech communities within the English-
language community, while in others the converse
evaluation obtains[64].

The grammatical (including phonological) rules
of a language system include only such as would
potentially be available to contemporary learners of
the language without benefit of historical knowledge.
Only materials that could be naturally collocated
within one system would be included, a statement whose
truth has to be accepted, even though little is yet
known about the (natural) limits of language systems.
Not all lects will be equally intelligible to other
lects, given the directionality of markings, implications, and the like, even in socially neutral contexts. But easy adjustments would be expected when
the users of the language move from one speech community to another. To be sure, those most familiar
with more leveled forms of English grammar would have
learning problems when they moved to communities where
less leveled forms of the language were frequent, and
these would be different from the problems encountered
by those moving from regions where less leveled varieties existed to regions where more leveled varieties
were frequent. Some would probably have to learn
more than others, as I have pointed out elsewhere[65].

New lexical uses would have to be learned by all, as
anyone who has served in the armed forces realizes.
New uses of items present in all varieties have to be
learned, and the absence of an item in one variety
presents problems for its speakers in other areas, as
well as conversely[6.6]

    An overall system is a union, rather than an
intersection, of subsystems. While it cannot be open-
ended if it is to be useful and meaningful for the
linguist, its limits need not be rigid (as envisioned
in Agard 1971), but can be left flexible. One must
distinguish the diverse effects of natural developments
from within and of mixture due to contact with other
systems. The internal mixing of subsystems is still
fairly lacking in sophisticated investigations, but
two notions may be tentatively put forward on the basis
of what little is known. Like cross-system mixture,
subsystem mixture results in leveling, e.g. the varieties of English found in the Midwestern and Western
States and BVE in Northern cities across the country
(even though in each specific city the contributions
from regional varieties of BVE have varied a great
deal)[6.7] Secondly, mixing of subsystems is not likely
(pace Sapir 160-1) to result in new systems, in the
manner that mixing systems is. I would reject the
term creolization for the mixing of subsystems within
a system, though not for mixing different components
(e.g. the lexicon) of different systems. Here the
term has a valid use.

    Studies of a large number of phonological rules
in English convinced me some years ago that rules can
not only be ordered implicationally, but that implications can branch off and form blocs within which
only language-users familiar with a particular over-all
type (perhaps dialect) would be expected to 'know' the
internal subimplications. As noted in Bailey 1972,
the whole bloc of implications may fill one place in
the implicational ordering of the rules for language-
users not familiar with the details of that bloc of
rules. As a result, the occurrence of any single rule
from the bloc in question would be equivalent to the
whole bloc for the outsiders.

    One problem that has received considerable atten-
tion in recent years may cease to be such a large problem in the polylectal framework: abstractness and

absolute neutralization (Kiparsky MS). For it would
seldom be the case that what was completely abstract
in one lect of the language system would be so in all
the others that a speaker-hearer would be familiar
with. In other words, even speakers for whom bad,
bared, bed, bid, and beard were alike in some style
would nevertheless normally be familiar with other
lects, and precisely other styles of their own pronunciation, in which the outputs were not neutralized[6,8]
Speakers of BVE who often neutralize then and den do
not over-correct den to then, as the monolectal assumption would predict, since the alternation [d] : [ð]
in then keeps [d] here apart from [d] in den. When
radio announcers over-correct noon to ['niᵘn], it is
precisely because they are aware that other lects do
not neutralize //u// and //ð// after //n//; they just do not
know which lexical items have which underlying vowel.

Not all variation is of course patterned. Besides
the non-identicalness of any two pronunciations of the
same word, even by a given speaker, Morgan (MS) suggests that situations can get so complex that the rules
simply are not prepared to handle them and break down.
The result is that a speaker unsystematically produces
an output that fits some aspect of the rule (e.g. an
agreement rule), but which may not be strictly in accord with the rule. This would be especially likely
where two rules might apply in similar situations; the
choice might simply be made randomly by a speaker.

4.1 The wave model. The isolects in Table 1 (in §3.1)
are temporally differentiated: the isolect generated
by the operation of rule 3a in environment a (i.e. mist
before a non-vowel) is prior to the one generated by
the operation of the rule in environment b (i.e. mist
before a vowel); this is prior to the isolect generated
by the rule in environment c (i.e. miss#ed before a
non-vowel); and this is in turn prior to the isolect
generated by the rule in environment d (i.e. miss#ed
before a vowel). Speakers intuitively know Principle 14,
which is a corollary of Principle 10a.[6,9]

(14) The operation of a rule in a lighter-
weighted environment implies its operation
in heavier-weighted environments. (If environment a is heavier-weighted than b,
and b is heavier than c, then: c ⊃ b ⊃ a.)

Relative time 0:   0

Relative time i:

Relative time ii:

Relative time iii:

Relative time iv:

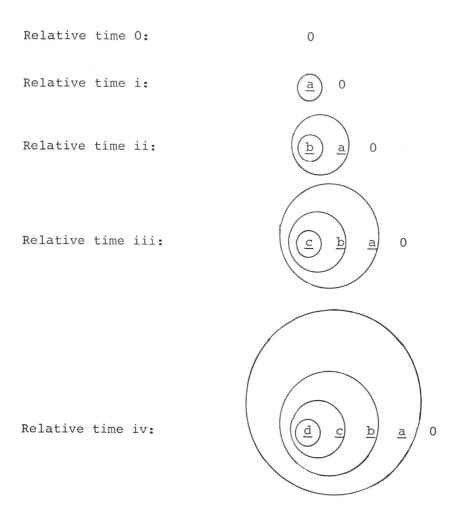

Fig. 2.   The Simplest Form of the Wave Model. (The
          letters represent successively later, or
          lighter-weighted, environments in which
          the rule operates.)

Fig. 2 portrays the spread of the isolects of
rule 3a through social space as a simple wave. The
wave is different for each relative time. Relative
times are defined on minimal (isolectal) changes.
Each new 'point' in social space results from 'cross-
ing' a single social barrier, i.e. from a single difference in social characteristics resulting from
differences in age, sex, social class, ethnic group-
ings, etc., including the urban/rural difference.
The point of origin is the point where the most recent
development has occurred--d̲ at time iv, c̲ at time iii,
etc. Fig. 2 is unaffected by the reweighting that
occurs in rule 3b; one simply substitutes environment
b̲' and c̲' of Table 2 for b̲ and c̲, respectively, in
Fig. 2. As a wave is propagated through social space,
it may have a different development (e.g. it may reweight at some point different from the origin) in one
direction from the developments found in other directions. (See table 8 in §4.2.)
    In order to bring Table 1 into accord with Prin-
ciple 8b in §3.2, each environment must begin variably,
as in Table 4. Fig. 3 represents this information in a
different manner from the portrayal of Table 1 in Fig. 2.

Table 4. Temporal development of isolects of rule 3a
          according to Principle 8b. (Variable ele-
          ments are parenthesized.)

Environment:	a̲	b̲	c̲	d̲
Time: Isolect:	mist##C	mist##V	miss#ed##C	miss#ed##V
i (a)	mis(t)	mist	missed	missed
ii (b)	mis(t)	mis(t)	missed	missed
iii (c)	mis(t)	mis(t)	miss(ed)	missed
iv (d)	mis(t)	mis(t)	miss(ed)	miss(ed)
v a	mis'	mis(t)	miss(ed)	miss(ed)
vi b	mis'	mis'	miss(ed)	miss(ed)
vii c	mis'	mis'	miss'	miss(ed)
viii d	mis'	mis'	miss'	miss'

Relative
time:

```
0        | 0
         ──────
         0

i        | (a) |
         |     |___ 0
         ─────────
         0   1

ii       | (b) |
         | (a) | (a) |
         |     |     |___ 0
         ───────────────
         0   1   2

iii      | (c) |
         | (b) | (b) |
         | (a) | (a) | (a) |
         |     |     |     |___ 0
         ─────────────────────
         0   1   2   3

iv       | (d) |
         | (c) | (c) |
         | (b) | (b) | (b) |
         | (a) | (a) | (a) | (a) |
         |     |     |     |     |___ 0
         ───────────────────────────
         0   1   2   3   4

v        | (d) | (d) |
         | (c) | (c) | (c) |
         | (b) | (b) | (b) | (b) |
         |  a  | (a) | (a) | (a) | (a) |
         |     |     |     |     |     |___ 0
         ─────────────────────────────────
         0   1   2   3   4   5
Lect:      a

vi       | (d) | (d) | (d) |
         | (c) | (c) | (c) | (c) |
         |  b  | (b) | (b) | (b) | (b) |
         |  a  |  a  | (a) | (a) | (a) | (a) |
         |     |     |     |     |     |     |___ 0
         ───────────────────────────────────────
         0   1   2   3   4   5   6
Lect:      b     a
```

Relative
time:

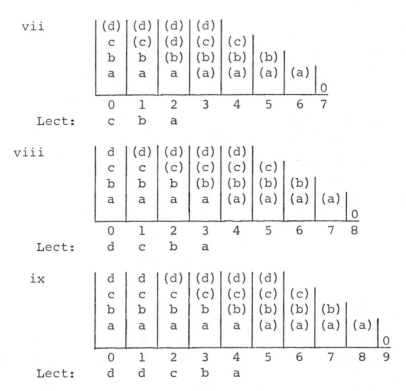

Fig. 3.   Propagation of Temporal Lects Shown in
          Table 4 Through Social Space.

        In Fig. 3 the vertical dimension is time; the
horizontal dimension represents points successively
remote from the point of origin (0) in social space,
i.e. points separated from the original lect by successively more social barriers. Variable environments
for the operation of rule 3a are parenthesized. At
times later than those shown here the pattern continues
rightward.
        Fig. 3 shows how to resolve the second static para-
dox (Becker 1967:64). Dialect geography shows that
rules get less general at the periphery of the areas
where they exist; but the logic of the acquisition of
language by children shows, as do many rule changes,
that rules get more--not less--general, i.e. by feature

Relative
time:

i | $(\alpha\ F_2,\ \beta\ F_1)$ |
                              0
    ‾‾‾‾‾‾‾‾‾‾‾‾‾‾‾‾‾‾‾‾‾‾
        0   1

ii | $(\alpha\ F_2,\ -\beta\ F_1)$ |
    | $(\alpha\ F_2,\ \ \beta\ F_1)$ | $(\alpha\ F_2,\ \beta\ F_1)$ |
                                                             0
    ‾‾‾‾‾‾‾‾‾‾‾‾‾‾‾‾‾‾‾‾‾‾‾‾‾‾‾‾‾‾‾‾‾‾‾‾‾
        0   1   2

iii | $(-\alpha\ F_2,\ \beta\ F_1)$ |
    | $(\alpha\ F_2,\ -\beta\ F_1)$ | $(\alpha\ F_2,\ -\beta\ F_1)$ |
    | $(\alpha\ F_2,\ \ \beta\ F_1)$ | $(\alpha\ F_2,\ \ \beta\ F_1)$ | $(\alpha\ F_2,\ \beta\ F_1)$ |
                                                                                       0
    ‾‾‾
        0   1   2   3

iv | $(-\alpha\ F_2,\ -\beta\ F_1)$ |
    | $(-\alpha\ F_2,\ \ \beta\ F_1)$ | $(-\alpha\ F_2,\ \beta\ F_1)$ |
    | $(\alpha\ F_2,\ -\beta\ F_1)$ | $(\alpha\ F_2,\ -\beta\ F_1)$ | $(\alpha\ F_2,\ -\beta\ F_1)$ |
    | $(\alpha\ F_2,\ \ \beta\ F_1)$ | $(\alpha\ F_2,\ \ \beta\ F_1)$ | $(\alpha\ F_2,\ \ \beta\ F_1)$ | $(\alpha\ F_2,\ \beta\ F_1)$ |
                                                                                                                       0
    ‾‾‾
        0   1   2   3   4

v | $(-\alpha\ F_2,\ -\beta\ F_1)$ | $(-\alpha\ F_2,\ -\beta\ F_1)$ |
    | $(-\alpha\ F_2,\ \ \beta\ F_1)$ | $(-\alpha\ F_2,\ \ \beta\ F_1)$ | $(-\alpha\ F_2,\ \beta\ F_1)$ |
    | $(\alpha\ F_2,\ -\beta\ F_1)$ | $(\alpha\ F_2,\ -\beta\ F_1)$ | $(\alpha\ F_2,\ -\beta\ F_1)$ |
    | $\ \ \alpha\ F_2,\ \ \ \beta\ F_1$ | $(\alpha\ F_2,\ \ \ \beta\ F_1)$ | $(\alpha\ F_2,\ \ \beta\ F_1)$ |
    ‾‾
        0   1   2

    | $(\alpha\ F_2,\ -\beta\ F_1)$ |
    | $(\alpha\ F_2,\ \ \beta\ F_1)$ | $(\alpha\ F_2,\ \beta\ F_1$ |
                                                              0
    ‾‾‾‾‾‾‾‾‾‾‾‾‾‾‾‾‾‾‾‾‾‾‾‾‾‾‾‾‾‾‾‾‾
        3   4   5

Relative
time:

vi

	$(-\alpha\ F_2,\ -\beta\ F_1)$	$(-\alpha\ F_2,\ -\beta\ F_1)$	$(-\alpha\ F_2,\ -\beta\ F_1)$	
	$(-\alpha\ F_2,\ \beta\ F_1)$	$(-\alpha\ F_2,\ \beta\ F_1)$	$(-\alpha\ F_2,\ \beta\ F_1)$	$(-\alpha\ F_2,\ \beta\ F_1)$
	$\alpha\ F_2,\ -\beta\ F_1$	$(\alpha\ F_2,\ -\beta\ F_1)$	$(\alpha\ F_2,\ -\beta\ F_1)$	$(\alpha\ F_2,\ -\beta\ F_1)$
	$\alpha\ F_2,\ \beta\ F_1$	$\alpha\ F_2,\ \beta\ F_1$	$(\alpha\ F_2,\ \beta\ F_1)$	$(\alpha\ F_2,\ \beta\ F_1)$
	0	1	2	3

$(\alpha\ F_2,\ -\beta\ F_1)$	
$(\alpha\ F_2,\ \beta\ F_1)$	$(\alpha\ F_2,\ \beta\ F_1$
	0
4	5 6

vii

	$(-\alpha\ F_2,\ -\beta\ F_1)$	$(-\alpha\ F_2,\ -\beta\ F_1)$	$(-\alpha\ F_2,\ -\beta\ F_1)$
	$-\alpha\ F_2,\ \beta\ F_1$	$(-\alpha\ F_2,\ \beta\ F_1)$	$(-\alpha\ F_2,\ \beta\ F_1)$
	$\alpha\ F_2,\ -\beta\ F_1$	$\alpha\ F_2,\ -\beta\ F_1$	$(\alpha\ F_2,\ -\beta\ F_1)$
	$\alpha\ F_2,\ \beta\ F_1$	$\alpha\ F_2,\ \beta\ F_1$	$\alpha\ F_2,\ \beta\ F_1$
	0	1	2

$(-\alpha\ F_2,\ -\beta\ F_1)$			
$(-\alpha\ F_2,\ \beta\ F_1)$	$(-\alpha\ F_2,\ \beta\ F_1)$		
$(\alpha\ F_2,\ -\beta\ F_1)$	$(\alpha\ F_2,\ -\beta\ F_1)$	$(\alpha\ F_2,\ -\beta\ F_1)$	
$(\alpha\ F_2,\ \beta\ F_1)$	$(\alpha\ F_2,\ \beta\ F_1)$	$(\alpha\ F_2,\ \beta\ F_1)$	$(\alpha\ F_2,\ \beta\ F_1)$
			0
3	4	5	6 7

viii

$-\alpha\ F_2,\ -\beta\ F_1$	$(-\alpha\ F_2,\ -\beta\ F_1)$	$(-\alpha\ F_2,\ -\beta\ F_1)$	$(-\alpha\ F_2,\ -\beta\ F_1)$
$-\alpha\ F_2,\ \beta\ F_1$	$-\alpha\ F_2,\ \beta\ F_1$	$(-\alpha\ F_2,\ \beta\ F_1)$	$(-\alpha\ F_2,\ \beta\ F_1)$
$\alpha\ F_2,\ -\beta\ F_1$	$\alpha\ F_2,\ -\beta\ F_1$	$\alpha\ F_2,\ -\beta\ F_1$	$(\alpha\ F_2,\ -\beta\ F_1)$
$\alpha\ F_2,\ \beta\ F_1$	$\alpha\ F_2,\ \beta\ F_1$	$\alpha\ F_2,\ \beta\ F_1$	$\alpha\ F_2,\ \beta\ F_1$
0	1	2	3

$(-\alpha\ F_2,\ -\beta\ F_1)$			
$(-\alpha\ F_2,\ \beta\ F_1)$	$(-\alpha\ F_2,\ \beta\ F_1)$		
$(\alpha\ F_2,\ -\beta\ F_1)$	$(\alpha\ F_2,\ -\beta\ F_1)$	$(\alpha\ F_2,\ -\beta\ F_1)$	
$(\alpha\ F_2,\ \beta\ F_1)$	$(\alpha\ F_2,\ \beta\ F_1)$	$(\alpha\ F_2,\ \beta\ F_1)$	$(\alpha\ F_2,\ \beta\ F_1)$
			0
4	5	6	7 8

Fig. 4. Another Version of Fig. 3, Employing Features.

deletions or value-generalizations. In Fig. 3, rules
do indeed get less general at points in social space
more and more remote from the origin, simply because
the earliness of the most limited environment for the
rule's operation ensures that it has had time to spread
farthest. But at any one point in social space the
rule indeed continues to become more general until it
is categorical (non-variable) in all environments, unless something causes the rule to die out before this
happens[70] This also explains the principle of the
antiquity of peripheral phenomena in areal linguistics.

     Two principles have been assumed in Fig. 3 and in
the discussion up to this point:
     (15) A single isolectal change creates a new
           relative time.
     (16) All the environments of a rule become
           variable before the oldest becomes
           categorical.
Principle 16 is probably not correct for all instances
(cf. Table 5 below), and supplementary algorithms will
be required. The principle is given here only tc provide a handle for the discussion. The correct algorithm for generating matrixes such as those shown in
Fig. 3 may require that the oldest (earliest, fastest)
environment become categorical in the isolect in which
the last environment begins to be (variably) operative.
This seems unlikely, as does the idea that variability
persists through a given number of isolects (equal,
perhaps, to the number of variable environments, as in
Fig. 3). The variability may well depend on clock time
in some manner. All such questions must be left for
future determination.

     Fig. 4 (p. 72) is a slightly more technical formu-
lation of Fig. 3 in terms of the variable features that
create the four environments of rule 3a. Note that, as
before, the lowest-number isolects are the oldest. See
Trudgill MS for interesting observations on models for
the diffusion of a change through social and geographical space.

     The same notations used in Fig. 3 are used in Fig.
F_2 is a feature that is heavier-weighted than F_1. At
each relative time subsequent to those shown here, each
isolect moves one step to the right.

     It is important to stress that language-users in-
ternalize language patterns, and that these, rather

than spatial distributions or statistical findings,
are what are of prime concern to the linguist. It
should be clear to the reader that the linguistic
pattern, viz. $\underline{C} \supset \underline{B} \supset \underline{A}$, is the same in both Fig. 5a
and 5b; that for what is linguistically relevant here
the bundling in Fig. 5b is of no importance, contrary
to claims of dialect geographers[7].[1] The importance of
such patterns, together with a corroboration of the
correctness of the wave model's predictions with regard to previously unknown data, has been demonstrated
in Bickerton 1971, where the patterning shown in Table 5
was verified. As for greater and lesser statistics
which language-users interpret and produce so competently
let us now turn to a discussion of how the wave model
and a couple of general principles account for this without the linguist's having to embrace the scarecely
credible view that children learn and internalize relative statistics.

Table 5. Isolectal distributions of the infinitive
          markers tu ('to') and fu ('for') in
          Guyana Creole English, adapted from
          Bickerton 1971. (The basilect is at
          time 0; the acrolect, at time vi. The
          isolect at time i was not attested in
          the data.)

	Verb classes:		
Relative times:	I	II	III
0	fu	fu	fu
*i	tu/fu	fu	fu
ii	tu	fu	fu
iii	tu	tu/fu	fu
iv	tu	tu	fu
v	tu	tu	tu/fu
vi	tu	tu	tu

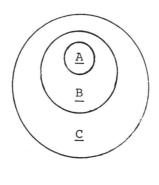

(a)

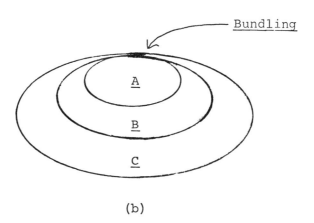

(b)

Fig. 5.   The Spatial Pattern, $C \supset B \supset A$, With 'Dialectal'
          Bundling in (b), But Not in (a).   (See fnn. 68
          and 71.)

Data which will be cited later show that incipient changes begin slowly, that after they get going they quickly pick up momentum, and that they begin to slow down as they near 100% categoricality. This forms an ∫-curve, as in Fig. 6. A principle like 17 governs this statistical distribution. There results the micromodel of statistical change seen as Fig. 7, which is adapted from the simpler model in Labov 1972:106; it illustrates the development of rule 18.

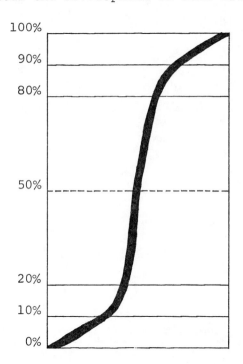

Fig. 6.   The ∫-curve generated by Principle 17.

(17)   A given change begins quite gradually; after reaching a certain point (say, twenty per cent), it picks up momentum and proceeds at a much faster rate; and finally tails off slowly before reaching completion. The result is an ∫-curve: the statistical differences among isolects in the middle relative times of the change will be greater than the statistical differences among the early and late isolects.

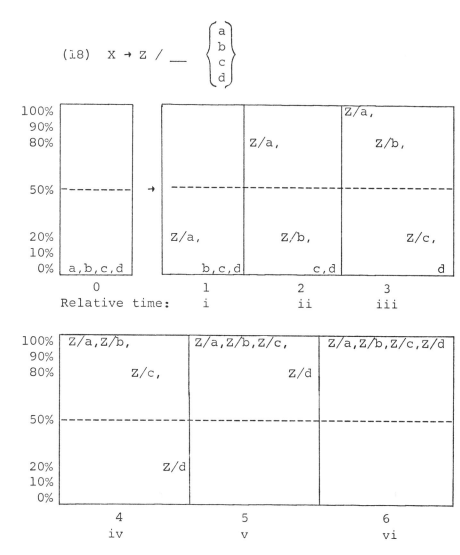

Fig. 7.   The Statistical Development of Rule 18.

The vertical dimension in Fig. 7 is that of increasing statistical implementation of the rule, as in
Fig. 6.   Time or space move rightward from the point
of origin, 0.   Isolects are represented by Arabic
numerals; relative times, by small Roman numerals.   The
notation Z/a means that the output is present in environment a in the percentage of possibilities indicated
on the vertical scale.

The application of the principles just discussed
to Fig. 3 results in Fig. 8. The application of Principle 10 in time and space, as in Fig. 8, presupposes
Principle (19):

(19a) At a given point in social space, the
       operation of a rule will be proportion-
       ately greater in earlier or heavier-
       weighted environments than in later or
       lighter-weighted ones.

(19b) A rule will operate in a given environ-
       ment proportionately more frequently--
       up to 100%--at points in social space
       nearer to the point of origin than at
       points more remote from the origin.

Env. d:	10%			
Env. c:	20%	10%		
Env. b:	80%	20%	10%	
Env. a:	90%	80%	20%	10%
Locale:	0	1	2	3
	Relative time iv			

Env. d:	20%	10%		
Env. c:	80%	20%	10%	
Env. b:	90%	80%	20%	10%
Env. a:	100%	90%	80%	20%
Locale:	0	1	2	3
	Relative time v			

Env. d:	80%	20%	10%	
Env. c:	90%	80%	20%	10%
Env. b:	100%	90%	80%	20%
Env. a:	100%	100%	90%	80%
	Relative time vi			

Env. d:	90%	80%	20%	10%
Env. c:	100%	90%	80%	20%
Env. b:	100%	100%	90%	80%
Env. a:	100%	100%	100%	90%
	Relative time vii			

Fig. 8. Application of Principle Under Discussion
         to Fig. 3.

In contrast with the increasing attenuation of physical
waves in time and space, the waves under discussion
show increasing strength in time (according to Principle 17), although at any given moment those parts
more distant from the origin than others will be
statistically weaker.

The wave-like nature of the statistics in Fig. 8 can be clearly seen in the breakdown of the figure at relative time v, shown here as Fig. 9. Exemplifications of something like Fig. 8 with real linguistic data are provided later on in Tables 9 and 10. These tables illustrate both the wave-like nature of the statistics and the ∫-curve of Principle 17.

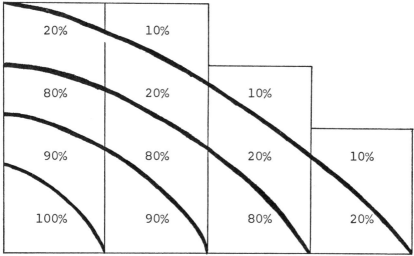

Fig. 9. Portrayal of Wave-like Nature of the Statistics in Fig. 8 at Relative Time v. (The wave loses its impetus at progressively more distant points in social space, at least in the relative statistics for any given moment.)

Cedergren & D. Sankoff (MS) have replaced Labov's emphasis on statistics with an emphasis on probabilities. This will certainly have a better chance of being a credible model of competence. One might hypothecate a universal (internal) bell curve or ∫-curve, and then seek to justify it; but learning complicated statistics will not be found credible. Probabilities are well-defined in a way that statistics are not; as Cedergren & Sankoff assert, "Frequencies are clearly part of performance, but we use them to estimate probabilities, which are part of the underlying model generating the observed behavior. It is our contention that these probabilities are properly part of competence." Of course, there is more to performance than a failure to achieve competence probabilities, as these writers are well-aware. Their proposals deserve further investigation, provided one thing is kept in mind. In the papers just cited, rules are provided with a static or fixed input probability, which is affected not only by variable factors in the linguistic environment, but also by variations of style, socio-economic class, and the like. These scholars have informed me that the input probability could be provided with a curve, thus creating vector-like dynamic rules that would generate the variety of patterns generated by Cedergren and D. Sankoff, but in a different way. Instead of generating them all at once, or instead of selecting a given speaker and setting his or her input probability at [some per-centage] depending on their socio-economic group and then calculating rule probabilities for each linguis-tic environment (see Cedergren and Sankoff), we would be more concerned with before-and-after relations among outputs, i.e. with generating all of the <u>linguistic</u> patterns of the language in the implicational sequence that holds valid for any speaker. Then, sociolinguis-tic algorithms of the sort proposed near the end of the present monograph could be applied for assigning the patterns so generated to the social parameters of a given speech community. A given pattern would be assigned to one style of a speaker in one class of the speech community, to another style of a speaker in another class, and so on. The linguistic parameters would be handled as proposed by Cedergren & D. Sankoff, but the input probability would ride on an $\int$-curve, so to speak. For recent discussion of related issues, the reader is referred to papers by Fasold, Bickerton, Wolfram, Cedergren, G. Sankoff, Anshen, and others in Bailey & Shuy 1973.

The writer's own difficulties with Cedergren and Sankoff's original proposals have to do not only with the static nature of the rules they have proposed and the failure to distinguish social from linguistic parameters, but also with the fact (not provided for in their proposal) that features are not independent. It is known that the values that promote or inhibit rule outputs may be quite different in lighter-weighted features according as the values of heavier-weighted features change. (Walt Wolfram has shown me some

quantitative data that make this statement indis-
putable; cf. Wolfram 1973.) None of these aspects of
the original proposals by Cedergren and D. Sankoff is
irremediable in their framework, and there is no reason
why their sophisticated techniques have to be incom-
patible with the program set forth here.

Principle 20 enables the language-user to interpret (and produce) statistics in accord with the patterns of data just shown, without the language-user's
having internalized (relative) numbers. The reader
should note the asymmetry between Principle 20 and
Principle 14, both of which are corollaries of Principle 10.

(20)   What is quantitatively less is slower
       and later; what is more is earlier and
       faster. (If environment a is heavier-
       weighted than b, and if b is heavier than
       c, then: a > b > c.)

My view is that the competence pattern is the temporally
created implicational one, which is perceptually deduced from the preceding principle.

Fasold 1973, agreeing on the perceptual principle, examines the issue whether an inferred earlier-
later principle is to be regarded as the correct competence principle. Fasold considers three cases in
which the quantitative implications and the temporal
ones disagree. The first of these is acceleration.
Fasold speaks of a rule accelerating ahead of another,
older one, but only cites instances of environments
or inputs accelerating. And he thinks that a given
instance of acceleration could occur at some point
in social space other than the origin. I used to hold
this view, but now think it highly unlikely. The difference in the forms of the wave for /æ/-raising in
the direction of New York City and in the westward
direction (discussed in §3.3) appears to be due to the
rise of new metropolitan centers of greater importance
than the one which the wave originally spread from.
Ordinarily, the time required for such new centers to
arise would far exceed the normal time required for
rules to reach completion (categoricality). Given that
reweighting or some other case of acceleration begins
at the origin of the wave, the effect is at some point
in time to rearrange the columns in a table like Table 4
above, as in Table 6 below:

Table 6.   A variant of Table 4 above in which a reweighting following time v transposes
columns b̲ and c̲.

Environment:		a̲	b̲	c̲	d̲
Time:	Isolect:				
i	(a)	mis(t)	mist	missed	missed
ii	(b)	mis(t)	mis(t)	missed	missed
iii	(c)	mis(t)	mis(t)	miss(ed)	missed
iv	(d)	mis(t)	mis(t)	miss(ed)	miss(ed)
v	a	mis'	mis(t)	miss(ed)	miss(ed)
vi	b	mis'	miss'	mis(t)	miss(ed)
vii	c	mis'	miss'	mis'	miss(ed)
viii	d	mis'	miss'	mis'	miss'

Note that if the reweighting which causes the acceleration of column c̲ ahead of b̲ does not occur precisely
when it does in Table 6 (see the broken line), it will
not be detectable in this chart. But Fasold contends
that in a quantitative chart (like Fig. 8 or Table 9
or 10) the statistics would be thrown off. I do not
think this would be the case provided the columns are
rearranged at the moment of acceleration in relative
time. (Note that the lect at the origin of the wave
is the one that is latest in time, viz. [d] in Table 6.)
Clearly, however, further investigation is in order,
with due consideration of the points made in Fasold's
article. The real question is, of course, how listeners would perceive the statistics: would they internalize the columnar transposition? Probably not, though
this applies only to those speakers having the reweighting, since the others could 'predict' such a reweighting and might be able to understand the columnar
transposition caused by it. I know of no principle
that would produce the acceleration of a later rule
ahead of an older one, though I do not doubt that while
both are still variable the later one would normally be
statistically farther from categoricality than the
older one. The one exception would occur when an older
rule became stagnant, but a later rule continued to
progress toward categoricality.

Since stagnant rules constitute Fasold's second
kind of discordancy between the quantitative and
temporal principle, these must be characterized now.
For up to this point the discussion of variation,
particularly the discussion of the $\int$-curve, has assumed
that rules proceed in time to completion, unless they
die out and cease having any effect on the grammar.
But in fact rules may freeze in mid course, so to speak,
like the rule affecting the alternation of interdental
fricatives and their corresponding stopped pronunciations in the lower middle class and the classes below
it in New York City (Labov 1966:365-372). Such a pattern may remain static for years. However, Principle
20 causes listeners to interpret even static rules in
vector terms. The frozen pattern represents the results of a time-differentiated spreading wave, so I
see no problems for Principle 20 here.

Fasold's third kind of problematic case involves
rule-inhibition. The rule desulcalizing //r// when not
prevocalic began in England as [- favored], but at
some point became [+ favored]; and it changed from
[+ favored] to [- favored] for most classes in New York
City at the time of World War II, as Labov 1966 shows.
(See discussion of [favored] in §4.4.) In the latter
example, older speakers simply have the rule in its
completed form; this is lect 0. Later lects show the
usual statistical developments, for Labov has shown,
both for this rule in New York City and for the rule
inhibiting the second output of rule 23 on Martha's
Vineyard, that the quantities which are charted for
rule-inhibition exhibit the same pattern as those in a
rule like rule 3. (See Table 9 below.) The statistics
for the inhibition of a rule still progressing toward
categoricality should present a chart something like
Table 7 if no changes occur in the form of the rule
(as in fact was the case on Martha's Vineyard). Note
that the inhibition of the rule does not disturb the
historical relations of more and less among the environments; i.e. it is inhibited more in the originally later
(lighter) environments than in the originally earlier
(heavier) environments.

If it is true that rule-inhibition does not disturb
the patterns of rule development, it will be necessary
to explain an apparent counterexample through reweighting or in some other way. The example in question

Table 7.   Presumed statistical relations in the
           development of a rule in earlier (a) and
           later (d) environments when a revaluation
           of the feature [favored] occurs following
           temporal lect 4.

Relative time:	Lect:	Age or other grouping:	Environments:			
			a	b	c	d
iii	3	IV	80%	20%	10%	0%
iv	4	III	90%	80%	20%	10%
v	5	II	80%	20%	10%	0%
vi	6	I	20%	10%	0%	0%

involves the change of /ɒ/ to /ɔ/, which seems
(McDavid 1940) to have reached the velar environment
last in the Southeastern States, but which is the
only environment where the change remains in the speech
of some speakers from the northern Pacific Coast States,
who have [ɔ] in dog and song, but [ɑ] in soft, cost,
and cloth. Despite this problematic example, other
instances of rule-inhibition known to the writer show
no disturbance in the pattern created by the development of the rule.
     A main point of Fasold's discussion fails to take
into account the difference between natural changes and
decreolization, a form of borrowing across systems.
The latter is governed by the decreolization or mixture
algorithm treated at the end of this monograph. The
wave model applies to such patterns as well as to others,
but Fasold may be right in maintaining that the relative
time of different developments is so obscured as to be
rendered meaningless in the difference between natural
changes and changes which reverse this order as mesolects in the creole gradatum mix with (by borrowing
from) the acrolect. Nonetheless, the implicationality
of the wave model is maintained--this is the main point
for the position taken in the present writing--and
there is no reason to suppose that the decreolizing
pattern obscures the directionality of natural changes

any more than rule inhibition in Table 7. See the
earlier discussion of decreolization in connection
with rule 3.

4.2 The variable rule for /ī/ in English. If the
brain is to be credited with the ability to deal with
the diverse patternings of the outputs of English /ī/
which the facts of communication demand, we must get
away from the facts of geographical and social[72]
repartitions of the variant outputs of this underlying
unit. As will be seen on the map in Fig. 10 below,
geographical dispersions can be so chaotic as to
challenge the plausibility of any hypotheses about
the orderliness of language variation and therefore
of any hypothesis about the brain's manner of storing
and using such variants in communication. In what
follows, such non-linguistic patterns will be reduced
to linguistic patterns, in which implicationally
adjacent isolects are placed side by side, regardless
of their geographical variation.
     Let us begin with the pattern from which the
others can be derived with principles already ex-
pounded. This pattern is that of the North of England,
with data from Kolb 1966. The social characteristics
of the informants for this data were kept as constant
as possible, so that the geographical variable should
be the only variable other than sex. Despite the
social uniformity in the sources of these data, the
resultant map (Fig. 10) is fairly chaotic.
     In Fig. 10, isolect numbers are the same as in
Table 8, but single parentheses indicate one deviation
from the pattern in that table, and double parentheses
denote two such deviations. Eighty-four sources of
data are represented on the map. Of a total of 672
items containing //ī//, 33--or less than 5%--are deviant.
Less deviance would probably result if sex differences
were controlled in the data. The broken line separates
the isolects having positive numbers or letters in
Table 8. The dotted line surrounds the lectal area
where geese is pronounced ['gəⁱs] or something similar.
This possibly represents the result of a reordering of
the sub-rules of the heavy-vowel shift (the one raising
mid nuclei to high nuclei, and the one raising low
nuclei to mid ones). The origin of the main wave is
Lincoln. The origin of the later wave appears to be
near Manchester (isolects B and C).

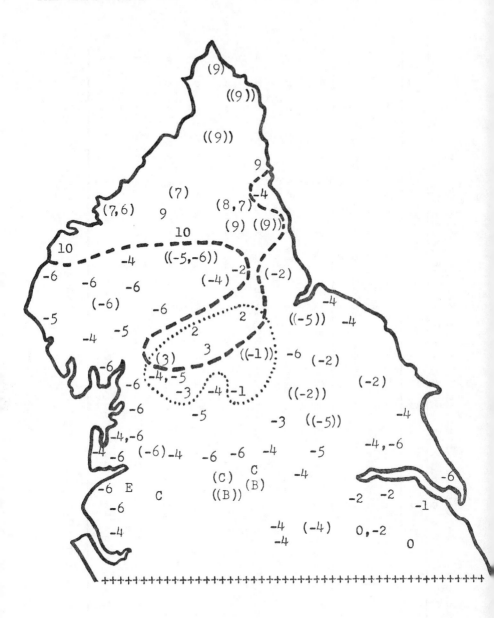

Fig. 10.   Isolects for the Outputs of ∥ī∥ in Dif-
           ferent Linguistic Environments as
           Distributed in the North of England.

Table 8. Pattern of linguistically adjacent isolects for the outputs of //ī// in the North of England

	*11	10	9	8	7	6	*5	*4	3	2	+1	0	-1	-2	-3	-4	-5	-6	*G	*F	E	*D	C	B	*A	*⊕
about		u	u	u	u	u	u	u	u / ɵu	u / ɵu	u / ɵu	u / ɑo	u	u	u	u	u	u	ɑo / ɑ	ɑo / ɑ	ɑo / ɑ	ɑo / ɑ	ɑo / ɑ	ɑo		
night	i	i	i	i	i	ɛi	ɛi	ɛi	ɵi	ɵi	Ei	æ	æ	i	i	i	i	i	i	i	i	i	i	i	i	ɑ
died§	i	i	i	i	i	ɛi	ɛi	ɛi	Ei	æ	æ	æ	æ	æ	Ei	i	i	i	i	i	i	i	i	ɑ	ɑ	ɑ
-wrìght	i	i	i	i	ɛi	ɛi	ɛi	ɛi	ɵi	ɵi	æ	æ	æ	æ	æ	Ei	i	i	i	i	i	i	ɑ	ɑ	ɑ	ɑ
writing	ɛi	ɛi	ɛi	ɛi	ɛi	ɛi	ɛi	ɛi	æ	æ	æ	æ	æ	æ	æ	æ	æ	æ	æ	æ	æ	æ	ɑ	ɑ	ɑ	ɑ
Friday	ɛi	ɛi	ɛi	ɛi	ɛi	ɛi	ɛi	ɛi	æ	æ	æ	æ	æ	æ	æ	æ	æ	æ	æ	æ	æ	ɑ	ɑ	ɑ	ɑ	ɑ
knife	ɛi	ɛi	ɛi	ɛi	ɛi	ɛi	ɛi	ɛi	æ	æ	æ	æ	æ	æ	æ	æ	æ	æ	æ	æ	ɑ	ɑ	ɑ	ɑ	ɑ	ɑ
time	ɛi	ɛi	ɛi	ɛi	ɛi	ɛi	æ	æ	æ	æ	æ	æ	æ	æ	æ	æ	æ	æ	æ	ɑ	ɑ	ɑ	ɑ	ɑ	ɑ	ɑ
sky	ɛi	ɛi	æ	æ	æ	æ	æ	æ	æ	æ	æ	æ	æ	æ	æ	æ	æ	æ	ɑ	ɑ	ɑ	ɑ	ɑ	ɑ	ɑ	ɑ

§Flies has been substituted for died in a few instances.

In Table 8 <u>Ei</u> indicates either the nucleus [ε^i] or the
nucleus [ə^i]. The wave from the origin (0) is generated with different algorithms to the left and to the
right. The isolects with negative numbers to the right
of the origin are generated by the 'normal algorithm'
and overlap with the later wave spreading from θ.
Unattested isolects are starred. These may turn up in
later data. Alternatively, there may be some kind of
higher-level (dialectal?) boundary between isolects 6
and 3 and between isolects -6 and E. The data are inadequate to test this matter because the later wave
overlaps and obliterates the ground of the older wave
(see the mapping of these data in Fig. 10). Note that
the [a] output of //ū// (in <u>about</u>) accelerates ahead of
the [a] output of //ī// in isolects -2, -4, and -6. Because the older isolects are closer to the origins,
the directionality of time sequencings must be read
<u>toward</u> the origins. Thus the isolects with [i] <u>-wright</u>
(as in <u>cartwright</u>) have not been completely affected
by the rule in question at the points where the wave
has arrived most recently.

The pattern as illustrated in Table 8 is generated
with rule 21, which assumes, on the basis of data from
other areas, that the prevelar environments are the
slowest of all.

$$(21) \begin{bmatrix} V \\ m \text{ phar. wid.} \\ m \text{ low} \\ 2 \subset \text{rhythmic length} \\ (u \text{ grave}) \end{bmatrix} \rightarrow \begin{bmatrix} \subset \text{ low} \\ M \text{ grave} \end{bmatrix} \begin{bmatrix} u \text{ nuclear} \\ \subset \text{ low} \end{bmatrix} /$$

$$\underline{\hspace{1cm}}([{*}m \text{ segmental}]) \left(\begin{bmatrix} c \\ 1 \subset \text{ lingual} \\ 3 \supset \text{ voiced} \end{bmatrix} \right)$$

Condition 1: At least one parenthesized element
              must be present in the environment.

Condition 2: $R_{\text{output peak}} > R_{\text{output satellite}}$
(R = rate) until the stage /a^a/ =
[a] has been reached.

Condition 3: In the North of England, the environment is absent for the outputs
of /ʊ/ when this input becomes
operative; input /ī/ or /ū/ is
still unchanged in older environments in the North of England.

We here extend the denotations of the implicational coefficients so that ⊃ denotes the order ↑, x, ↓ where
gradient values are involved, while ⊂ denotes the
reverse sequence. See feature 36 in the Appendix.
   In rule 21, the input has two variable features;
where no implicational coefficient or weighting numeral
is present, variability is indicated by parentheses.
The feature [⊂ rhythmic lengthening] causes paroxytonic
environments (e.g. Friday, writing) to show later outputs than their corresponding oxytones (e.g. died,
write), in accordance with the data under analysis.
Input [(u grave)] ensures that changes of input /ū/ lag
behind those of /ī/ (see on the acceleration of /ū/
ahead of /ī/ in England below). The input feature,
⌈pharyngeal width⌉, is somewhat doubtful.[7,3] Condition 2
ensures that the lowness of the output satellite lags
behind that of the peak until the last stage is reached
the outputs for front inputs therefore are: (i) /ε^i/
or /ə^i/, the difference between which is ignored here
in favor of the latter; (ii) /a^e/; (iii) /a^a/ = [a].
In the output, the feature [round] retains its same
absolute values as in the input, but becomes marked in
the output /ə^u/, which explains its later unmarking to
/ə^u/ and /a^o/. Probably it unmarks and reassimilates
in lects having /ə^u/. (The writer favors Chomsky and
Halle's 1968:419-435 view of linking, despite the
criticisms in Bach and Harms 1972, where the possibilities of distinguishing lower-level and higher-level
unmarkings are not realized.) To see why the change of
[u grave] or [m grave] inputs to [M grave] is not unnatural, it is necessary to re-examine Table 8. There
it is obvious that /ə^i/ does not occur in lects lacking
changes of input /ū/, which are later than changes of
/ī/. The compromise [M grave] position--central instea
of either front or back--is presumably a higher-level

unmarking that overrules feature-unmarking; see Principle 1b in §3.0.

When the optional variable [*m segmental] (that
is, a syllabic boundary) is present in the environment,
the asterisk indicates that the rule categorically
generates the latest output found in the lect in question. The data provide evidence only for sky, but
evidence in other lects suggests that the formulation
of 21 is correct. (Note that in Kolb's data the rule
operates in Friday, so that a # following /d/ does not
need to be posited for the rule here, as it does in
other lects.)

The sequencing of the outputs of /ū/ parallels
those of /ī/: /eᵘ/ or /əᵘ/, /aᵒ/, /aᵃ/ = [a], as in
mouse. In the North of England, the environments of
the rule appear to have little effect on the distribution of the environments — speakers apparently using
some given output for all words in a given style of
speaking.

The sequencing of the segmental environments in
rule 21 depends, as usual, on the relative weightings
of the features in the environment and on [rhythmic
length] in the input segment. The weighting [⊂ lingual]
ensures that labial environments are faster than apical
ones, while velar environments are slowest of all. Although the data offer no evidence for velars, these
form the slowest environment in all other lects for
which there is evidence. In English /ī/ precedes //g//
only in tiger, Geiger, Nygren, and migratory (and words
having the same base form as this last); /ū/ does not
occur before grave consonants at all. Within each
category formed by a value of [lingual], [⊂ rhythmic
length] generates a given output in an accented syllable
followed by unaccented syllables in the same word prior
to generating that output in oxytonic syllables. Thus,
Friday and writing change before died, flies, and night.[7,4]
Within each combination of [lingual] and [rhythmic
length] values, underlying voiced consonants provide
faster environments than underlying voiceless consonants.

Table 8 shows two patterns for intersequencing outputs and environments. The normal algorithm sequences
the two outputs of the original wave, [əⁱ] and [aᵉ], in
each environment before moving to the next, as in isolects 0 through -6. In all attested isolects shown on
the right of 0 in Table 8, [aᵉ] has already been

generated in the five heavier-weighted environments.
Another algorithm is evidenced in the isolects on the
left of isolect 0, since the five heavier-weighted
environments have [ɛⁱ] before [aᵉ] is generated in the
heaviest, and then [ɛⁱ] is successively generated in
the lighter-weighted environments before [aᵉ] begins
to be generated in all but the heaviest one. It is
no great task to devise ad hoc rate indices for such
intersequencing, and such notations probably have to
be resorted to until more general principles governing
the intersequencings are discovered. There would be
no point in complicating rule 21 further, so the 'non-
normal' algorithm for intersequencing will be left for
future research.

Table 8 shows that in isolects -2, -4, and -6 the
output [a] has been generated for input /ū/ before it
has been generated for input /ī/. This could be provided for in rule 21 by generalizing the next variable input feature, [u grave], to [m grave] according to Principle 9a. Principle 10b would then ensure
that, after an interim, the [m grave] input, /ū/, would
be affected prior to /ī/ in the wave spreading from
the latter origin.

Besides the treatment of /ī ū/ found in the North
of England--and the oldest speakers on Martha's Vineyard (Labov 1972a)--there are several other important
treatments of the inputs, differing chiefly in the
environment of the rule. In the standard pronunciation
of English in Scotland at the time of the first World
War, many speakers (Grant 1914:63) had the second-stage
or /aᵉ/ output of /ī/ only before //r z ð v// and #;
contrast <u>tide</u> ['thaⁱd] with <u>tie#d</u> ['thaᵉd]. This suggests that the boundary feature at the beginning of the
environment in rule 21 should have been some other
feature defined so that the value denoting a syllabic
boundary could generalize to the value denoting an
internal word boundary. Grant says that a syllabic
boundary following the nucleus favors /aᵉ/. And apparently /əᵘ/ is not heard in the variety of speech
described by Grant, which shows that the [m grave] input has accelerated ahead of the [u grave] input, according to Principle 10b. What is to be said of the
non-lateral continuants environing the Scots form of
rule 21? Evidently there are two possibilities:
(1) The original panlectal form of the rule had the

appropriate features, but very lightly-weighted originally, and then these were reweighted to greater importance in Scots. While the North of England data do
not offer the required evidence, the similar pattern
among older speakers on Martha's Vineyard (Labov 1972a:
122) does show light fricatives less favorable to /əi/--
and therefore more favorable to the later output, /ae/--
than stops are. (2) One can easily envision a paradigmatic generalization of a word boundary from <u>die</u> to
<u>died</u>. In fact Grant points out that the variety of
English being described sometimes had ['wəivz] as the
result of leveling the pronunciation of <u>wives</u> to that
of <u>wife</u>. This last example does not, of course, involve
a boundary, but the kind of generalization involved is
the same as in <u>die</u> and <u>died</u>.

    This problematic lect will not be dealt with fur-
ther here, but rather our attention will be turned to
some lects that seem related to it. In various areas
of New York State, Pennsylvania, and Virginia (and
probably elsewhere), there are speakers that have
/ae aᵒ/ in <u>bribe</u>, <u>ride</u>, <u>loud</u>, <u>down</u> and elsewhere when
the environing consonant is immediately followed by #,
as in <u>briber</u>, <u>rider</u>; contrast /əi/ in <u>fiber</u>, <u>cider</u>,
<u>spider</u>. (Note here that it is a # following the en-
vironing consonant that is important, and not just
simply a # preceding it, as in the Scottish speech described above.) The rate of environments is: oxytones
with environing light consonants other than //g// are
fastest; paroxytones with # intervening before the unaccented syllable that follows are next; and paroxytones
without # following the environing light consonant are
slowest. This is just the opposite of what was found
in the North of England, where <u>Friday</u> is a faster environment than <u>died</u> and <u>flies</u>. The influence of the #
following the environing consonant is attributable to a
paradigmatic generalization often found in language.
The priority of the change in <u>bribe</u> and <u>ride</u> over <u>fiber</u>,
<u>cider</u>, and <u>spider</u> might conceivably be explained thus:
Let us assume that the original (panlectal) rule had
[m = ↓ rhythmic length] instead of [⊂ rhythmic length]
in the input. Now, if this has already generalized to
[α rhythmic length] in the lects under consideration,
Principle 10b would dictate the priority of [M = ↑
rhythmic length] inputs. Unfortunately, there is no
concrete evidence of [α rhythmic length] in these lects.⁷˒⁵

Labov's (1972) spectrographic data show a change
from a pattern similar to that of the North of England
among the oldest speakers on Martha's Vineyard to a
pattern similar to what is found in the Southern States
(including most of the Tidewater areas) among younger
speakers in Martha's Vineyard. Here ⌈voiced⌉ has become the heaviest-weighted feature, while [rhythmic
length] has only vestigial importance.[6]   Both ⌈u grave⌉
and [m grave] inputs, i.e. /ī/ and /ū/, are affected by
the rule, now formulated as 22. This rule has evolved
naturally out of 21 simply by reweighting [voiced].
For reasons that go beyond the present state of knowledge on the subject, the [m grave] inputs have not
accelerated ahead of the [u grave] inputs, according to
Principle 10b. (See below, however, for the acceleration in nineteenth-century England.) There is some
question as to whether the final change--of /a^e a^o/ to
/a^a/ = [a]--is part of the rule or some other, since
the fastest environment in the Southern States, as in
Southern England,is before the back-vowel satellites
/ɨ ɹ ə/, as in <u>tile</u>, <u>tire</u>, <u>owl</u>, <u>hour</u> (see Fig. 11).[7]
This contrasts with the fact that the velar environment
(e.g. <u>tiger</u>) is the last light-consonant environment to
be affected by the rule. It may be that the change of
rules 21 and 22 actually began in the environments preceding satellites derived from the underlying liquids,
and then spread as a crazy-rule generalization to other
environments. One can provide for the early change before these satellites by adding [ɔ nuclear⌉ as the
heaviest-weighted feature in the segmental environment
(cf. also Labov 1972a:122). If this feature belongs in
the Southern States rule, rule 22, it also belongs in
rule 21.

Since rule 22 is related to rule 21 by natural
developments, speakers of at least these varieties of
English presumably have the panlectal rule in their
competence. It remains to be tested whether users of
English in the North of England understand those in the
Southern States more readily than the reverse. But in
view of the fact that speakers of different lects of
English (other than more or less recent creoles) communicate with one another after a brief acclimatiza-
tion, it would defy common sense to inveigh against a
unified grammar generating the lectal variants under
discussion. Idiolectal formulations would militate

against the communicative fact that we deal with and
know a lot more of our language than the small parts
of it that we produce in our manifold styles.

$$
(22)
\begin{bmatrix}
V \\
m \text{ pharyg. wid.} \\
m \text{ low} \\
4\subset \text{ rhythmic length} \\
(u \text{ grave})
\end{bmatrix}
\rightarrow
\begin{bmatrix}
\subset \text{ low} \\
M \text{ grave}
\end{bmatrix}
\begin{bmatrix}
u \text{ nuclear} \\
\subset \text{ low}
\end{bmatrix} /
$$

$$
\underline{\quad} \; ([*m \text{ segmental}])
\begin{pmatrix}
\begin{bmatrix}
1\supset \text{ nuclear} \\
2\supset \text{ voiced} \\
3\subset \text{ lingual}
\end{bmatrix}
\end{pmatrix}
$$

Condition 1: At least one parenthesized element
              must be present in the environment.
Condition 2: $R_{output\ peak} > R_{output\ satellite}$
              until the stage /a[a]/ = [a] has been
              reached.
Condition 3: In the Southern States, no input is
              unchanged; in the Tidewater areas,
              the stage /a[a]/ has only been reached
              in allegro styles before satellites.

	0	1	2	3	4	5	6	7	8	9
about	a about	æo about	æo about	æo about	əo about	əo about	əu about	əu about	əu about	əu about
loud	a loud	æo loud	æo loud	æo loud	æo loud	əo loud	ɑo loud	ɑo loud	ɑo loud	ɑo loud
hour	a hour	a hour	a hour	æo hour	æo hour	əo hour	əo hour	əo hour	ɑo hour	ɑo hour
night	a night	a night	ae night	ae night	ae night	ae night	əi night	əi night	əi night	əi night
tiger	a tiger	a tiger	ae tiger	ae tiger	ae tiger	əi tiger	əi tiger	əi tiger	əi tiger	əi tiger
time	a time	a time	a time	a time	a time	a time	a time	a time	ae time	əe time
tire	ɑ tire	a tire	a tire	a tire	a tire	a tire	a tire	a tire	a tire	ɑe tire

Fig. 11. Isolects for /ī ūʲ/ in the Southern States.

0 – Unattested? 1 – Substandard general. 2 – Semistandard general. 3 – Standard general. 4 – Standard Deep South. 5 – Richmond, Alexandria. 6 – Fredricksburg, Lexington. 7 – Raleigh, Columbia. 8 – Norfolk, Wilmington; with ɑː Beaufort. 9 – Charleston.

In Fig. 11, <u>tile</u> is like <u>tire</u>; <u>try</u>, like <u>time</u>; <u>hike</u>, like <u>night</u>; <u>fowl</u>, like <u>hour</u>; and <u>cow</u>, like <u>loud</u>. Since the wave is spreading from its origin in the direction of the arrow, the temporal developments are to be read in the opposite direction, from right to left toward the origin.

Fig. 11 shows that the algorithm for interse-quencing input changes, output differences, and environ-ment differences is extremely complex. Isolects 3 and 4 are created by changes on the input $/\!/\bar{u}/\!/$, while the other isolects are created by changes on the input $/\!/\bar{i}/\!/$. Isolects 4, 5, and 6 are created by changes yielding a diphthong with a low-vowel peak, but the other isolects are created by changes resulting in the satellite-less nuclear output [a]. And assuming the correctness of Fig. 11, isolects 3 and 8 are created by the rule's operation in the heaviest environment, viz. before $/\!\!\!\!\frown \; \dot{1}/$; only isolect 7 shows the effects of the next-heaviest environment, viz. a word boundary or an under-lying voiced non-velar segment; isolects 2 and 6 are generated in the environment formed by a following $/\!/g/\!/$; and the lightest environment, the one where an under-lying voiceless obstruent follows, is operative in creating isolects 1, 4, and 5.

Other developments of rule 21 can be summarized briefly. In the Midwestern and Western States, as well as in British RP, the outputs [a^e a^o] (with retracted or raised peak vowel in some regions) appear in almost all environments. In other words, the environment has been almost completely generalized, i.e. eliminated. However, the change of /a^e a^o/ to /a^a/ = [a] occurs among some Midwesterners and many Southern Englishmen before the satellites $/\dot{1} \; \sigma \; \vartheta/$. Jones (1964:106-107, 110-111) cites British RP reductions in the environ-ments in <u>fire</u>, <u>hire</u>, <u>society</u>, <u>violin</u>, <u>trial</u>, <u>power</u>, <u>our</u>, <u>towel</u>, and <u>vowel</u>, but excludes the reductions (at least in moderate tempo) in <u>high#er</u>, <u>dy#er</u>, <u>plough#er</u>, <u>allow-#able</u>, <u>allow#ance</u>, and (exceptionally) in <u>coward</u>. One should also note the evidence (cited in Chomsky and Halle 1968:284) that in the early nineteenth century in Southern England the output of the [m grave] input had accelerated ahead of that of the [u grave] input, exactly as Principle 10b specifies, since /a^o/ existed in the faster environments while /a^e/ did not yet exist.

Two summarizing remarks can conclude this section.

Despite differences among Southerners in the United
States and despite the differences in outputs and
conditions on the operation of the rule diphthongizing
(and monophthongizing again) the outputs of underlying
//ī ū// which have to be specified between Southerners
and North Englanders and Midwesterners in America, all
the patterns can be reduced to a single panlectal rule,
though not without different algorithms here and there
for intersequencing the effects of different parts of
the rule. This makes a panlectal grammar feasible,
for these data are as complex as any to be met within
a language which indeed possesses (at least in some
lects) a supercomplex phonology.

The other part of this summary involves dialect
geography. First, it is obvious that Table 8 tells us
more about the language than Fig. 10, which only portrays chaos. Nevertheless, the kind of mapping illustrated in Fig. 10 greatly mitigates the greater chaos
of older isoglossic approaches. It also, in combination with a table like Table 8, has the great advan-
tage of permitting us to locate the origin of a wave of
change, i.e. by locating the home of the isolect with
the greatest developments.[7,8] The fact that in the
Southern States the wave of changes to /a/ in the
faster environments (and from /ǝⁱ eᵘ/ to /aᵉ aᵒ/ in
the slower ones) is located well inland from the
Atlantic Coast and has 'backed up' toward the coast
indicates that the direction of this change has been
in the opposite direction from the direction of migration (from the coast inland). This makes the emphasis
on migration routes in previous dialect studies of
questionable value. Incidentally, the High-German consonant shift, which spread northward from the South,
moved in a direction opposed to that of migration. One
does not yet know just how general this phenomenon is.

The writer hopes to have demonstrated the validity
of his claim that the study of variation has a lot to
contribute to linguistic theory and to have substanti-
ated the feasibility of polylectal formulations. In
place of dialectology, now on the periphery of theoretical linguistics, the writer would put lectology in
the center of linguistics and insist that it perform
the job that dialectology was originally charged with
many years ago, viz. to tell us how language works.

4.3 <u>Overlapping waves</u>. The first proposal of a wave
theory was by Schmidt (1872). Though lacking a wave
model, Schmidt's evidence for waves and against family
trees was conclusive and reads fresh today. His other
works indicate that he ranks with Saussure as a syste-
matizer, far surpassing the theoretical talents of the
German Neogrammarians. From now on, linguists will
surely rank Schmidt and Schuchardt above the latter
when it comes to theory. What one finds in a so-called
family tree of, say, Indo-European is a group of language systems each containing some proportion of Indo-
European ingredients--much less for Tokharian and
Albanian than for Greek and Sanskrit, with other languages ranged on a scale between these poles. Each
such system contains another proportion, greater as the
Indo-European proportion is lesser, of ingredients from
other, non-Indo-European ancestors. The view already
expressed earlier is that natural changes caused by
children acquiring a language--unmarking, generaliza-
tion--will never create a new system. This is created
by heterosystematic mixture. Thus, every legitimate
node (every node representing a new system) on a so-
called family tree must have two or more parents.

Mixture among the lects of a system is always
present, and probably only rarely absent among language
systems. Mixture, lexical and otherwise, between Old
English and French (itself filtered from Latin through
Keltic, Frankish, and Norse) produced Middle English.
How thorough-going this was may be discerned from three
formatives which are Germanic in form but Romance in
function: <u>wh</u>-relatives, <u>-ly</u> adverbs, and <u>-ing</u> pro-
gressives (see further Bailey 1973a). And today we
witness 'foreign' formations like denominative adverbs
in <u>-wise</u>. (These were hardly modeled on English forms
like <u>otherwise</u>, which are de-adjectivals.) What makes
English so adaptable as a world language is its continuing adaptability to creolization.

Table 8 has already shown the interaction of two
parts of the same rule propagated as waves from earlier
and later points of origin. Schmidt 1872 made it clear
that language systems show the effects of overlapping
waves, at least on the lexical level. Whatever is said
now about the effects of competing waves is of course
speculative, in view of the lack of the requisite factual
data. Fig. 12 gives an idealized scheme of the overlapping of competing waves. The symbol 1 represents the

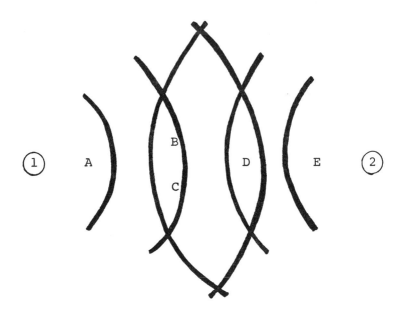

Fig. 12.   Idealized Scheme of the Manner in
            which Competing Waves Overlap.

origin of rule 1; and 2, the origin of rule 2.   The
marked ordering of the rules has 1 prior to 2.   The
idealization assumes that the rate of propagation of
the two rules through social space is the same.   The
capital letters designate different lects.   Lect E
possesses only rule 2, and lect A possesses only rule 1.
The other lects have both rules.   In lect B rule 2
arrives after rule 1; the result is the marked order,
1, 2.   It is just the opposite in lect D, where the unmarked order, 2, 1, obtains.   Lect C stems from B by
way of a reordering of the rules to their unmarked
order, 2, 1.   Thus lect C is just like lect D, though
the reasons are different for the ordering in the two
lects.   Presumably a lect *F would be impossible if it
involved changing the unmarked rule order of lect E to
a marked one, since this violates Principle 1a.
    It is obvious that differences in the rate of
propagation of the two waves would have to be taken
into consideration in a real-life situation.   Whatever
differences may exist between the interaction of

tautosystematic rules and heterosystematic rules are
of course unknown. But given the normality of creolization in language, the matter requires further ex-
ploration by variationists who are expert in creolization. In the end, it might be possible to clear up
the vexed questions concerning a possible Balto-Slavic,
Italo-Keltic, or other proto-language.

4.4 Algorithms for converting unilinear implicational
patterns into multidimensional sociolinguistic patterns
in a speech community. The panlectal rules of a language community generate various patterns which are
handled differently in the speech communities defined
by such treatments of the patterns. Where Labov defines
a speech community "as a group of people who share a
common set of norms about language" (cf. fn. 63), I
would rather characterize it in terms of the evaluations
(the feature is [favored]) and the sociolinguistic algorithms which assign the unilinear series of implicational outputs of a variable rule to sets characterized
by different social parameters. And in fact Labov's
(1973:59) most recent published view is that "the
crucial issue for pan-dialectal grammars is not understanding or evaluation, but prediction."

The present discussion presupposes that rules have
features. A language-community rule feature might be
[↑ tempo] or something similar, to indicate that the
rule operates more often as the tempo increases. A
speech-community feature is [favored]. In a given
speech community a [- favored] rule is inhibited in
more monitored styles, while the same rule would be
preferred in monitored styles in speech communities
where it is marked [+ favored]. Non-variable rules
are [x favored], i.e. neither favored nor disfavored.

Before discussing the sociolinguistic algorithms,
it may be helpful to illustrate with a simple example
what is involved. Fig. 13 shows the wave-like spread
(cf. Fig. 14) of a series of four implicationally arranged outputs of a variable rule across a bidimen-
sional matrix from one relative time to another. The
small letters denote progressively later environments,
as well as those implied by them according to Principle
14 (not all of which will necessarily still be variable).
The small Roman numerals stand for relative time steps.
The capital letters and the capital Roman numerals may

Time 0	A	B	C	D	i	A	B	C	D	ii	A	B	C	D	iii	A	B	C	D
IV	-	-	-	-		-	-	-	-		-	-	-	-		a	-	-	-
III	-	-	-	-		-	-	-	-		a	-	-	-		b	a	-	-
II	-	-	-	-		a	-	-	-		b	a	-	-		c	b	a	-
I	-	-	-	-		-	-	-	-		a	-	-	-		b	a	-	-

Time iv	A	B	C	D	v	A	B	C	D	vi	A	B	C	D	vii	A	B	C	D
IV	b	a	-	-		c	b	a	-		d	c	b	a		+	d	c	b
III	c	b	a	-		d	c	b	-!		+	d	c	-!		+	+	d	a
II	d	c	b	a		+	d	c	b		+	+	d	c		+	+	+	d
I	c	b	a	-		d	c	b	a		+	d	c	b		+	+	d	c

Time viii	A	B	C	D	ix	A	B	C	D	x	A	B	C	D	xi	A	B	C	D
IV	+	+	d	c		+	+	+	d		+	+	+	+		+	+	+	+
III	+	+	+	b!		+	+	+	c!		+	+	+	d!		+	+	+	+
II	+	+	+	+		+	+	+	+		+	+	+	+		+	+	+	+
I	+	+	+	+		+	+	+	+		+	+	+	+		+	+	+	+

Fig. 13. Covariation of Two Social Parameters in the
Temporal Development of a Disfavored Change
that Begins in the II-A Cell of Matrix i.
(The exclamation point is explained in
algorithm 5 below.)

stand for steps on any two social or stylistic scales
whose steps are coordinated with relative time steps.
The parameter represented by I, II, III, and IV and tha
designated A, B, C, and D could be any sociological
dimensions that serve as barriers to the spread of the
wave through social space, provided that these barriers
are coordinated with one relative time. The vertical
dimension may represent successively higher social
classes from I to IV; and the horizontal dimension may
represent increasingly monitored tempo or style differences. The matrices for different relative times may
also represent different points in social space (cf.
Fig. 3 in §4.1). Changes may apparently originate in
any segment of a social community, but until a re-
evaluation (cf. the originally lower-class 'broad-a'

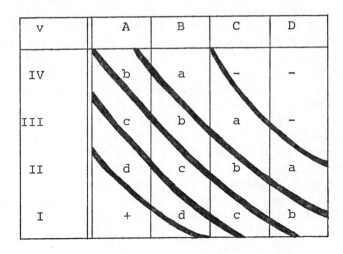

v	A	B	C	D
IV	b	a	-	-
III	c	b	a	-
II	d	c	b	a
I	+	d	c	b

Fig. 14. The Matrix for Time <u>v</u> from
Fig. 13, Shown as a Wave
Spreading Across Social Space.

in England) occurs, changes originating in the lower
or lower-middle class are normally [- favored], while
those originating in the upper class are [+ favored].
A [x favored] change is one that is not evaluated;
this includes some variable rules. Only variable rules
are amenable to the sociolinguistic algorithms to be
presented below, although categorical rules may differ-
entiate social classes as well as any other. A point
to be noted in connection with the evaluation of a linguistic phenomenon as favored (prestigious) or disfavored (stigmatized) is that group solidarity may
cause a [- favored] feature of language to become
[+ favored] in certain social situations, and conversely.
Differences in future aspiration may have a like effect
on [favored]. This effect may be so great that friends
of the same social class going to the same school on
Martha's Vineyard or in Silver Spring, Maryland, may
grow up with different 'accents'. Of the two kinds of
linguistic changes, the kind that begin in unmonitored
speech (perhaps first as slips of the tongue) may be
favored or disfavored, but most of those that begin in
monitored speech (over-corrections) will probably be
favored changes, though pronouncing the 'w' in <u>sword</u> or
<u>answer</u>, the 't' in <u>often</u> or <u>soften</u>, and similar spelling

pronunciations are likely to be viewed as simple ig-
norance. Note that the 'ng' in the gerund is viewed
by the middle classes as much superior to 'dropping
the 'g''.

Variable linguistic data will fit a table like
one of the matrixes in Fig. 13 if the social dimensions which are selected are ones that covary with
time steps. This usually has to be ascertained for a
given rule by trial and error. Thus, Labov (1966:
279) found that differences in the 'social class',
constituted of occupational and educational factors,
made the best fit in his study of variation in the
pronunciation of the initial consonants of thin and
then. Other class differences fit other situations
better, including hereditary status, ethnic, religious,
and economic differences. Thus, Labov found ethnic
correlations in his study of the raising of /æ/ and
/ɔ̄/. The best fit for 'r-ful' variation in New York
City was obtained with the 'socio-economic class',
including salary, occupational, and educational factors.
The statistics that resulted from the 'r-ful' study are
shown here as Table 9, where four 'styles' are shown to
covary with the socio-economic class. Table 9 differs
from Fig 13 in two ways. The statistics do not represent separate linguistic environments (like a, b, c,
and d in Fig. 13), but all environments. Further, it
is a [+ favored] phenomenon that is shown in Table 9.
It originates in the upper right-hand corner.

In Table 9, the numbers on the left designate
successively higher socio-economic classes, while the
capital letters designate successively more formal or
more monitored styles. The data are from Labov 1966:221;
the cross-over of the second highest class is not shown
in this arrangement of the data. The differences between the average statistic of each wave are greater at
the lower left than elsewhere, thus confirming the ∫-
curve stipulated by Principle 17.

The knowledge about his language which a language-
user must possess in order to interpret or produce
speech in accord with the statistics of Table 9 consists of Principles 14 and 20 and knowledge of whether
the phenomenon is favored or disfavored. This last may
have to await the end of adolescence for full attainment. Although the ages of 12±1 and 18±1 are linguistic
turning points in our culture, many age factors are only

Table 9.	Percentages of inhibition of the desulcalization rule, shown as a wave spreading across the style-class matrix.				
Styles:	A	B	C	D	D'
Classes:					
6-9	12.5	25.0	29.0	55.0	70.0
3-5	4.0	12.5	21.0	35.0	55.0
0-2	2.5	10.5	14.5	23.5	49.5

accidentally relevant to a given variable rule. The
age of 40 in Labov's study of 'r-fulness' in New York
City was quite arbitrary. It took into account the
time of World War II and of the influx of Midwesterners
into New York City in managerial positions in great
numbers. The difference between male and female or between urban and city-dweller can often be fitted into
matrixes like those we have been looking at as relevant
social dimensions that covary with time differences in
the data. Factors affecting style other than tempo and
familiarity are status and topic differences. Many of
these have been investigated.

It has to be assumed that each band of the wave in
Table 9 is a separate isolect. So important statistical
differences are to be regarded as a kind of minimal difference delimiting isolects. It has relevance to the
author's definition of a speech community, that different bands in a statistical matrix should constitute
different isolects; and the sociolinguistic algorithms
as such are relevant to the concept.

The division of the socio-economic classes in
Table 9 obliterates the cross-over of the second highest
class which Labov has stressed so often. Another class
division with six strata (Labov 1966:240) yields the
cross-over. It is provided for in the algorithms given
later.

Table 10. Percentages of deletion of the lateral consonant for four groups of four Montrealers; from Sankoff MS, Table 2.				
	Professionals		Working Class	
	Women	Men	Women	Men
il (impersonal)	94.7	98.5	100.0	[99.4]
ils	67.7	88.4	100.0	100.0
il (personal)	54.0	[90.0]	100.0	100.0
elle	29.8	[29.7]	74.6	96.4
les (pronoun)	16.0	25.0	50.0	78.1
la (article)	3.8	15.7	44.7	49.2
la (pronoun)	0.0	[28.5]	33.3	[50.0]
les (article)	[5.4]	13.1	21.7	34.6

Table 10 differs from Table 9 in portraying three, rather than two, sociolinguistic dimensions. Discrepant figures are placed in square brackets. The clearly discernible wave spreading across the table has not been drawn in here. Note, as in Table 9, that the statistics are more bunched in the bottom and top percentages and more spread out towards the middle percentages; i.e. the differences between the average figures of the wave bands are less in the lower left and upper right corners than in the middle of the table. Even greater numbers have been used (e.g. Labov et al. 1968:i, 149) than are used in Table 10. The difficulties in portraying larger numbers of social and linguistic dimensions in rule variation shows the need for algorithms that will convert a unilinear series like e ⊃ d ⊃ c ⊃ b ⊃ a or a > b > c > d > e into such multidimensional matrixes. These are easy enough to formulate, given a knowledge of the relevant points on the scale of each dimension which covary with time steps. They are purely relative, assuming we are already at a point in a unilinear implicational series--defined for a given set of sociolinguistic characteristics--and wish to know where in that series some other set of sociolinguistic characteristics would be.

In the sociolinguistic algorithms that follow, alpha indicates either plus or minus (but only one or the other throughout the formula). The value +1 isolect indicates a move to one isolect or band in a statistical wave which is temporally more distant from the origin. Conversely, -1 isolect denotes a change to one isolect or band in a statistical wave which is temporally nearer the origin. The accumulation of several differences will result in several steps (forwards, backwards, or both) in time. See the example given below.

1. Move $\alpha 1$ isolect for $\alpha 1$ younger relevant age grouping, and $-\alpha 1$ isolect for each older one.

2. Move $\alpha 1$ isolect for [α female] sex of speaker. Rules in other cultures, and perhaps even some in our culture, will require [α male] for the algorithm to operate correctly.

3. Move +1 isolect for each class farther from the class in which the change originated. (See also algorithm 5.)

4a. If the change is [+ favored], move +1 isolect for each more monitored style and -1 isolect for each less monitored style.

4b. If the change is [- favored], move -1 isolect for each more monitored style and +1 isolect for each less monitored style.

Note that degrees of formality (styles, effected by different values of [monitored], which is probably a gradient feature; see fn. 54) are varieties of social distance, no less than class, age, and sex differences. Since a [+ favored] change first enters the speech of a given set of social parameters in its most monitored style--and conversely for [- favored] changes, which enter in the least monitored style--we do not get the picture of a fully developed wave (as in Fig. 13) until the change has spread through all the styles. At first we will find breaks (see Table 11), as the change affects only one, or at least not all, of the styles in the speech of a typical speaker of a defined set of social traits. Note that the sociolinguistic algorithms operate only for typical speakers, since socially deviant individuals may well speak the lect of some other social group. Note also that it is society, not a string of rule outputs, that is multidimensional--the argument against using social factors in rules.

Table 11.	Portrayal of the spread of a [+ favored] change having two environments in two styles, three age groupings, and three classes. (The change commences in the monitored (M) style of each group and later spreads to the unmonitored (U) style.)					
Age group:	Grandparent		Parent		Grandchild	
Styles:	U	M	U	M	U	M
Upper class	–	a	a	b	b	+
Middle class	–	–	–	a	a	b
Lower class	–	–	–	–	–	a

5. <u>The cross-over of the second-highest class</u>[7,9]
In this class, for [α favored] changes, move α2 isolects in changing from a non-reading style to an adjacent reading style, and -α2 isolects in changing from
a reading style to an adjacent non-reading style.
See Fig. 13.
It has already been noted that considerations of
group solidarity or future aspirations may reverse the
coefficient of the feature [favored]. Note that the
move is 0 isolect if the feature for a difference is
[x favored], i.e. neither favored nor disfavored.
Let us suppose that a speaker is a female of the
lower-middle class using style C, and that we know
where she stands on the scale. To ascertain where a
male in the next older age grouping and the next higher
class would be for a [+ favored] change, we simply move
toward the origin one isolect each for his maleness and
his older age and then one isolect away from the origin
for his class. After these three isolectal steps we
would then move two away from the origin if the older
male were speaking in style D.
If in place of the dimension represented by the
values of the feature [favored], we substitute an acrolect, a mesolect, and a basilect in a decreolizing
gradatum, we find the interesting nature of polysystematic mixture exhibited in Table 12. This mixture is

Table 12.   Pattern of mixture in a decreolizing gradatum.

Linguistic Environments:		The Language Community (Natural changes)			
		a	b	c	d
A Speech Community (Learned differences)	ACROLECTAL SYSTEM Z is a [- favored] item.	Z Z Z Z	Ø Z Z Z	Ø Ø Z Z	Ø Ø Ø Z
	MESOLECTAL GRADATUM Y is peculiar to the mesolects.	Y,Z Y X,Y X X X	Z Y,Z Y X,Y X X	Z Z Y,Z Y X,Y X	Z Z Z Y,Z Y X,Y
	BASILECT X is a basilectal item.	X	X	X	X

not random, but is governed by an algorithm that requires
the order of items in the social (vertical) dimension to
be preserved in the linguistic (horizontal) dimension.
In some gradatums X,Y,Z might be found in place of Y
standing alone in a given environment in the mesolects.
If Z in the acrolect is a [+ favored] item, the pattern
will be different. For data illustrating the implicational nature of such mixtures, cf. Bickerton MS. What
is relevant to the present discussion is that the mixture
accords with the patterns generated by a wave model; and
therefore sociolinguistic algorithms similar to those
discussed above are applicable also in situations where
polysystematic mixture is involved. What the interrelations of different types of phenomena in the overall pattern might be is something too complex to consider at the
present time. It will be a fertile field for future investigation.

APPENDIX: FEATURE MARKING & WEIGHTING

In the view of the present writer, phonetic markings
depend on the position of a segment in a syllable.
This approach is syllable-sensitive or syllable-
dependent and therefore different from most views
which have been put forward heretofore.

Sources for ascertaining which feature values
are unmarked (u̲), marked (m̲), or overmarked (M̲) include rule changes (of the sort that do not involve
higher-level unmarkings and may result in increased
feature-marking), implicational distributions among
languages of the world, and--where the evidence is
clear and accordant with the foregoing--the order in
which children in their post-babbling stage of language acquisition acquire the features of a language
system (the marked being later than the unmarked).
There may be in addition considerations of physiological production of sounds or of acoustical similarities and differences. Before giving the details
of feature markings, the ternary-valued features accepted in the present writing may be listed as follows:
1. [pulmonic]
       + pulmonic air source, always u
       x glottal air source, always m
       - velaric or palatar air source, always M
2. [egressive]
       + egressive air stream, always u
       x both egressive and ingressive (some
         labial-velars), always M
       - ingressive, always m
3. [voiced]
       + voiced, u for non-obstruents, m for obstruents
       x voiceless, m for non-obstruents, u for
         obstruents
       - aspirated, always M
   Kim (1970) has proposed that the voicing feature is

really a feature denoting the size of the glottal opening. (I would have used the feature name
[glottal opening], except that [voiced] has come
to be too well-known to make it worthwhile to
substitute a new term.)

4.   [pharyngeal widening]
+ wider pharynx, u for vowels in open syllables
(see fn. 60) and sonorant consonants, m for
vowels in closed syllables and for obstruents
x neutral, u for vowels in closed syllables but
m for vowels in open syllables and for sonorant
consonants, u for obstruents
- narrowed pharynx (pharyngealization), always M
Because of a resyllabication that occurs in English
between the first bloc of rules and the greater
number of rules that follow (Bailey MSb, MSc), English surface phonetics have an expectation of
[+ pharyngeal] vowels in open and in loosely closed
syllables (those closed with only a weak cluster
not followed by two weakly accented syllables in the
word) and [x pharyngeal] vowels in tightly closed
syllables (those closed because of a heavy cluster
following the nucleus or because of two following
unaccented syllables). These facts suggest that
perhaps [length increment] (see feature no. 25 below) would be a more appropriate feature than
[pharyngeal width]; but fn. 73 shows that there is
a difference between nuclear decrements due to
following heavy obstruents and nuclear shortening
due to following unaccented syllables. (In an
accent-timed language like English, an accented syllable has to be shorter when unaccented syllables
intervene before the next accented syllable and
perceptually are more so as more unaccented syllables follow.) As for consonants, it is believed
that [pharyngeal width] is the cause of differences
in air pressure, so that a feature ⌈air pressure⌉
is not required.

5.   [thyroid]
+ raised larynx, always M
x neutral, marking values as for [x pharyngeal]
- lowered, marking values as for [+ pharyngeal]

6.   [laryngeal]
+ creaky voice, always M
x murmured (breathy voice), always m
- no laryngealization, always u

7. [whisper]
    + stage whisper, always M
    x plain whisper, always m
    - unwhispered, always u
8. ⌐nuclear⌐
    + syllabic peak (see discussion of values below)
    x satellite of compound nucleus (unsyllabic nuclear)
    - non-nuclear
9. [turbulent]
    + obstruents (see discussion of values below!
    x semiturbulent or deflected air stream: sonorants
    - non-turbulent: low and mid accented vowels
10. [continuant]
    + continuants: fricatives and liquids other than taps (see discussion of values below)
    x semicontinuants (non-steady-state continuants and semi-stops): glides, the glottal stop, taps, nasal sonorants[80]
    - occlusives (including [^{n}d t^s t^l t^h], but not [^{d}ɍ̌])
11. [released]
    The value of this feature for consonantal and nuclear diphthongs is unclear; see below.
12. [nasal]
    + fully nasalized (see discussion of values below)
    x partially nasalized, always M (found in Chinantec and in those kinds of English that distinguish apple from ample as [x nasal] and [+ nasal], respectively).
    - non-nasal
    Perhaps a feature, [air pressure], will also be needed.
13. [liquid]
    + lateral (see discussion of values below)
    x grooved (see [sulcal] below)
    - undeflected oral air stream
14. [sulcal]
    + narrow-grooved, u for sibilants (- nuc, + trb, + cnt, = sul) in non-special positions (see below), m for sibilants in special positions, M otherwise

      x wide-grooved, u for high vowels and sibilants
        in special positions (as in Portuguese lects
        and Swiss German), m otherwise
      - non-sulcal, u for non-high vowels and non-
        sibilants, M for sibilants

15.   [vibrant]
      + trilled (see discussion of values below, and
        also see ⌈release⌉)
      x tapped or flapped
      - non-vibrant

16.   [grave]
      + back rounded vowels and labial(ized) velars,
        rounded labials (including ⌈w⌉), and velar-
        ized apicals or labials (see discussion of
        consonantal values below); always m for
        accented vowels and M for unaccented vowels
      x central and back unrounded vowels and un-
        rounded velar, postvelar, and labial con-
        sonants; always M for accented vowels and u
        for unaccented vowels
      - front vowels and apical and palatal con-
        sonants; always u for accented vowels and m
        for unaccented vowels.

Since this feature does not distinguish unrounded
back and central vowels, [+ grave] may have to be
made to include all back vowels. See Figs. 15 and
16.

17.   [lingual]
      + dorsal or rhyzolingual (see discussion of values
        below)
      x apical
      - labial

18.   [low]
      + low vowels, always u for accented and M for un-
        accented vowels (perhaps used for glottal con-
        sonants with m value)
      x mid vowels, always M for accented vowels and u
        for unaccented vowels (perhaps used for uvular
        and labial consonants with M value)
      - high vowels, always m (perhaps used for dorsal
        and apical consonants with u value)

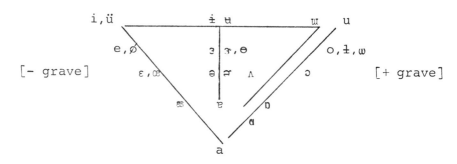

Fig. 15.   Schematization of values of [grave]
           for vowels.

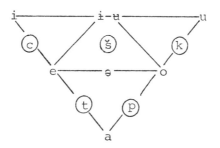

Fig. 16.   Possible allocation of values of [grave] for
           vowels and consonants. (Because of the prob-
           lems for consonants, these values have not
           been adopted in the system of features pro-
           posed in this writing.)

19. [dorsal]
        + convex dorsum (dorsals), u for all vowels (see
          discussion of values in consonants below)
        x dorsum neither convex nor concave, M for vowels
        - concave dorsum (retroflex articulation), m for
          vowels (e.g. [ᵾ̴])
        Note the following distinctions:

	[+ dor]	[x dor]	[- dor]
[+ sul]	[ʂ]	[s]	[ş]
[x sul]	[š̬]	[š]	[ș̌]

20.   [round]
        + over-round, in-rounded, or more-rounded,
          always M
        x plain rounded, u for high back bowels, [w],
          [r], and wide-grooved sibilants
        - unrounded, u for other vowels and consonants
      To account for the assimilation of [s] to round-
      ing when adjacent to a labial consonant in Eng-
      lish, [x round] might also refer to labiality,
      reserving [+ round] to [b^W m^W] and the like.
      Note that English [w] is more-rounded, as in
      <u>woo</u>, whereas classical Latin [w k^W] and earlier
      English [w] were [x round] and therefore swal-
      lowed up in following rounded vowels.
21.   [coronal]
        + apical, u for [x lng] consonants, M for
          vowels and other consonants
        x laminal, m for [x lng] consonants and all
          sibilants, m for vowels
        - non-coronal, u for vowels, [x̄ lng] consonants
22.   [dental]
        + predental or addental (values depending on
          foregoing), u for non-vibrants
        x alveolar (gingival), u for trills
        - neither, always u for all segments except
          [x lng] consonants other than trills
23.   There may be a feature [peripheral], but this is
      not certain; it would be a purely phonetic (i.e.
      non-phonological feature).
24.   [accent], a purely phonological feature
        + fully accented, m for vowels
        x mid-accented, M for vowels
        - accented, u for all segments
25.   [length increment]
        + length increment (rules may add several such
          increments), M for vowels, m for consonants
        x neutral, u for all segments

- length decrement, m for vowels, M for consonants
Note that a length increment can be added to
others cumulatively, as in 'r-less' <u>bird</u>
['bə:·d].
26. [tune increment]
    + ↑ increased pitch, loudness, and duration,
      u (from [+ addressee-oriented])
    x neutral, M
    - ↓ decreased pitch, loudness, and duration,
      m (used for foregrounding, imperatives, and
      compounding; foregrounding includes initial
      <u>wh</u>-elements), m (from [- addressee-oriented])
The arrows denote gradient values. The feature
[rhythmic length] (no. 36) is not to be con-
fused with [↓ tune increment].
27. [raised pitch limit]
    ↑ raised upper pitch limit, m (from [+ vivid])
    x neutral
    ↓ raised lower pitch limit, m (from
      [+ tentative])
28. [amplification]
    ↑ amplified ranges of pitch, loudness, and tempo
      (= retardation), m (from [+ high-lighted])
    x neutral, u (from [x high-lighted])
    ↓ contracted ranges of pitch, loudness, and
      tempo (= acceleration), M (from [- high-
      lighted])
29. [cadence]
    + falling unaccented syllables at end of phono-
      logical phrase, u (from [+ conclusive])
    x level, M (from [+ sinister] or [x conclusive])
    - rising, m (from [- conclusive], which is in
      turn generated from various features)
30. [jagged]
    + jagged envelope with unaccented syllables
      [- upper], u
    x jagged envelope with unaccented syllables
      [+ upper], M
    - envelope not jagged, m
This is probably a purely phonological feature,
whose values are respectively derived from the
force features, [+ assertive, - assertive,
x assertive].

31. [smooth]
         + smooth envelope, with unaccented syllables
           averaged between surrounding pitches, m
         x stair-step envelope, with unaccented syl-
           lables on same pitch as preceding accented
           syllable, M
         - neither (i.e. jagged), u
     This feature has its values derived respectively
     from [- detached, + detached, x detached].
32. [kinetic]
         + bidirectional pitch gliding, M
         x unidirectional pitch gliding, m
         - unglided, u
     Kinetic tones with one vertically long and one
     vertically short glide (i.e. ╱╲ ╱╲ ╱) are
     to be treated as compound tones (pivoted compounds
     with both sides vertically long do not exist).
     In most languages, kinetic tones which are pivoted
     and have one side vertically long are compounded
     of unpivoted kinetic tones; but in some languages,
     it may be that the compound represents a [+ upper]
     or [- upper] pivoted tone and an unpivoted kinetic
     tone in the other part of the pitch range.
33. [upper]
         + upper two-fourths of pitch range, m
         x middle two-fourths of pitch range for non-
           glided tones, u; entire four-fourths of pitch
           range for gliding (kinetic) tones, M
         - lower two-fourths of pitch range, M for un-
           glided tones, u for kinetic tones
     This feature is derived from several others; note
     that presupposed information is [- lower].
34. [rising-start]
         + rising-start kinetic tone, m
         x level (non-kinetic) tone, u
         - falling-start kinetic tone, M
35. [rhythm]
         + accent-timed, M
         x syllable-timed, u (often found in pidgins;
           cf. also fn. 24)
         - neither
36. [rhythmic length]
         ↑ gradient lengthening, M
         x no lengthening or shortening, u
         ↓ gradient shortening, m

This feature is phonetically dependent on [rhythm]
but is needed in phonological rules like rule 21
above. Its marking values depend on those of
[rhythm], but have not been worked out here.
37. [segmental]
    + segment (not a boundary), u
    x syllabic boundary, m
    - other boundary, M
38. [word boundary]
    + internal word boundary (#), M
    x morpheme boundary (+), m
    - neither of the foregoing, u

Before explaining features not defined above like
[release], it may clarify matters to point out that
phonetic [ph hp ^{n}d ^{d}ř t^l d^ž p^f a^e ə^i] and the like may
derive from phonological units or from two phonological
segments. Thus, English [ʋ^I] in fluid derives from
/uı/ (cf. fluidity), but [a^o] in loud derives from the
underlying unit /ū/. And English [d^ž] derives from
/dy/ in verdure and didya, but from the phonological
unit /g/ in regent (cf. regal). The feature [release]
may be helpful for designating phonological units from
which there are generated more than one phone (e.g.
/^{n}d ^{d}ř p̆/), provided onsets are distinguished from off-
sets. (The aspiration feature has to be used in con-
juncation with [release] for /^{h}p/ and /p^h/.) It is
assumed that nuclear peaks would have homorganic peripheral releases if marked [+ release]; e.g. /ə^i ə^u/.
The mid-value could be used for in-gliding, or else to
distinguish /a^e ₐ^o/ from /a^i ₐ^u/. One might respectively distinguish /^{d}ř/ from a tap from a trilled /ř/
as [x release], [- release], and [+ release], but
problems are involved in this course.[8.1] As for /bh/
and the like, it is well-known that one may not use
the aspiration feature; possibly such phonological segments could be designated as both murmured and aspir-
ated, but this is unclear.
    Here follows a discussion of the values of [nuc,
trb, cnt, grv, lng, dor] and, as a group, [nas, liq,
vib, sul]. The special positions mentioned below are
the position following a tautosyllabic accented syllabic peak and the position preceding a tautosyllabic
prevocalic consonant. Only the first of these is

relevant to [cnt], but both are relevant to the place
features [grv, lng].

The values of [nuc] are [+,u nuc] for the peak,
where no other value is possible; [x,u nuc] for a
satellite of the peak; obstruents can only be ⌐-,u nuc⌐,
except for those unusual cases of syllabic sibilants
([+,M nuc]). But the values of sonorants can range
over all three values of [nuc], depending on the environment; hence the specification of these values is
iterative. The unmarked values of [nuc] can be ascertained from the study by Bailey and Milner 1968, where
they are posited for the binary feature, [syl] (syllabic). This statement depended on the evidence of
Indo-European in the alternations referred to as Sievers-
Edgerton's Law (not valid after the internuclear loss
of the so-called laryngeals). But compare modern French,
where [y] is preferred to [i] in the environment heard
in rien, whereas [i] is preferred to [y] in that heard
in triomphe. In English [x nuc] is grouped with [+ nuc]
as [= nuc], but in PIE it was grouped with [- nuc] as
[+]nuc].

To understand the values of [cnt], it is necessary
to begin with the syllabic peak--[+,u cnt], unless a
compound nucleus or syllabic nasal ([x,m cnt]), [-,M
cnt] being impossible--and work away from it in both
directions. One then establishes the values for the
segments preceding and following the peak; after which
the values of the segments farther from the peak are
relative to the next segment nearer the peak, [- cnt]
alternating with [= cnt] as the unmarked situation for
all consonants except in the prevocalic cluster [sn]
(see fn. 83). Except for the peak and the special
position immediately following it, [x cnt] is [M cnt].
The values for the segments next to the peak are:

Prenuclear:	Post-peak (special position):
[-,u cnt]	[x,u cnt]
[x,m cnt]	[+,m cnt]
[+,M cnt]	[-,M cnt]

The values of the other non-nuclear segments depend on
what is found in the positions just described:

<table>
<tr><td>Prenuclear:</td><td>Postnuclear:</td></tr>
</table>

Before [-,u cnt]: [+,u cnt][82]   After [x,u cnt] or
             [-,m cnt]   [+,m cnt]: [-,u cnt]
                                 [+,m cnt]

Before [x,m cnt] or   After [-,M cnt]:
 [+,M cnt]:[83] [-,u cnt]   [+,u cnt][84]
            [+,m cnt]   [-,m cnt]

The immediately preceding definitions must be applied
iteratively as one proceeds away from the nuclear peak.
    To understand the remaining features, it is neces-
sary to note the expectations for the occurrence of
different segments in different environments, but especially in the special position following the peak of
the syllable. Here glides are more expected than nasals,
nasals more than liquids, liquids more than fricatives,
and fricatives more than stops. Thus, [x cnt] is
[u cnt] here, [+ cnt] is [m cnt], and [- cnt] is
[M cnt]; and [x trb] is [u trb], while [+ trb] is
[m trb], and [- trb] is hardly possible, given the
limit of one peak per syllable. Except for fricatives,
where [s] is expected in all positions, velars are more
expected than labials, and these more than apicals, in
the special position. Thus velarized liquids and glides
are preferred to others in the special position following the nucleus, but not elsewhere. Of the liquids,
/r/ is preferred to the lateral everywhere (including
the peak position) except at the beginning of a syllable
or following [s] (note the relative rarity of /tl skl
sr/), though a tap is preferred to a trill syllable-
finally. (Note the change of pl, gl, etc., to pr, gr,
etc., in Portuguese.) The features designating the
liquids must therefore have the appropriate values to
ensure these expectations. In the non-special positions,
apical non-fricatives are preferred to labials, and
these to velars; this accounts for the prenuclear and
postnuclear matathesis of /tp/ and /tk/ in various languages. Palatals are regarded in the following markings
as being, like labialized velars, unexpected segments in
the special positions, except when the result of assimilation, a higher-level unmarking process. (Note the
change of underlying // // to [l] in Spanish aquel.)

Non-special positions:

More expected: Apicals: [-,u grv, x,u lng, x,u dor]

                Labials: [x,m grv, -,m lng, x,u dor]

                Palatals: [-,u grv, +,M lng, +,u dor]

Less expected: Velars: [x,m grv, +,M lng, +,M dor]

Special positions:

More expected: Velars: [x,u grv, +,u lng, +,u dor]

                Labials: [x,u grv, -,m lng, -,u dor]

                Apicals: [-,m grv, x,M lng, -,u dor]

Less expected: Palatals: [-,m grv, +,M lng, +,m dor]

Note that the values of [lng] and [dor] are relative to
and dependent on the heavier-weighted feature, [grv];
this is true of [lng] only in the special positions.
In languages like English, where post-peak glides are
[= nuc], glides ([x trb, - nas, x cnt]) are part of the
nucleus and therefore unpermitted in the special positions, which may still be occupied by other sonorants,
at least in the postnuclear part of the syllable. In
languages where glides are [≠ nuc], the [+ grave] glide
[w] is preferred in languages having only one glide in
this environment, just as [- grave] [y] is preferred
before the vowel in languages having only one glide in
this environment. Where both glides occur as satellites, it appears that the unmarked one is [w] after
back or central vowels and [y] after front vowels.
Where palatals occur, laminopalatal sibilants are more
expected than the pure palatals and are to be marked
[x,u dor].[85] Such segments are then less marked than
labials in the non-special positions--possibly indicating an incorrect feature analysis--and no more marked
in the special positions than apicals. This must be
left as a problem for further investigation here. (Note
that the metathesis in classical Attic Greek of /ny ry/
to /ⁱn ⁱr/ after /a o/ does not prove that palatals are
preferred to apicals in the postnuclear special position,
since glides are preferred to other sonorants there.)
While some languages have syllable-initial [ŋ] but not
[ɲ] and other languages exhibit syllable-initial [ɲ]

but not [ŋ], the only way to resolve the issue of
which is preferred in this position is to assume that
the velar is preferred and to set up underlying ⫽ny⫽
or something similar for [ɲ], ruling out palatals in
all underlying representations.

The marking values for fricative obstruents have
been indicated only for the sibilants thus far. Presumably, as with other consonants, labials are more
expected than velars in the non-special positions,
while velars are more expected than labials in the
special positions. The palatal, bilabial, and interdental fricatives are rarest; the former presumably
results only from the higher-level unmarking process
of assimilation, while the interdental fricatives presumably arise only in the higher-level unmarking process of chain shifts. The place features have to
depend on the combination of [+ trb, + cnt] and then
have to be calculated for fricatives to insure the
foregoing results.

Sometimes boundaries classify with consonants in
rules; at other times, they classify with vowels.
Some provision should be made for this in a feature
system.

It is important to observe in connection with the
writing of rules that the abbreviations V (vowel) and
C (consonant) may sometimes abbreviate quite complex,
even bracketed, environments. But the abbreviations
certainly seem justified in terms of language-users'
competence. As is well-known to all who have been
extensively engaged in writing rules with marking feature values, some of these rules are much simpler and
others are much more complex than rules utilizing absolute (plus and minus) values.

For feature-stripping and for correlations of
various prosodic phenomena with unmarked rhythm and unmarked syllabication, see fn. 24. Thus, [h] is often
preferred to [s] in the special position. Note that
when a more marked phenomenon (e.g. a uvular trill)
replaces a less marked one (e.g. an apical trill) as
the result of borrowing, it is still incumbent on the
linguist to posit a natural origin for the marked phenomenon. Uvular trills may be presumed to begin in the
environment of segments with lowered uvula, and in fact
they often begin in languages having nasal vowels (e.g.
French, Portuguese); they can then spread to other

environments by a crazy-rule generalization (cf. Bach
and Harms).

The reader is warned against the frequent con-
fusion of <u>unmarking</u> with <u>leveling</u>. Maximizing feeding
order, but not minimizing bleeding order, results in
leveling. Mixture often results in leveling, but also,
as in the preceding example, results in an increase of
markedness; cf. also the borrowing of [m voiced] word-
initial fricatives into Old English from French.

Besides Saussure himself, a number of scholars
have discussed hierarchies of strength among features
or sounds: Hoenigswald MS, Foley, 1970, Vennemann
1972a, Chen MSb, Friedrich 1971, and Zwicky 1972; cf.
also Krohn 1969. Various approaches are possible to
determine the relative weightings. I have mainly used
reweighting changes (first discovered by Labov 1969);
cf. the exposition of rule 3b in §3.1. This often con-
verges with the results of other approaches. One is to
regard features as less heavily weighted than others
on whose markings their own markings depend when they
are bundled together in a single segment. Feature
values which are implied by others in the phonological
inventories of natural languages offer a good mode of
determining relative weightings, but frequency in languages of the world may be a less secure criterion.
Very important is the order in which most children acquire features systematically (cf. fn. 16), i.e. after
the babbling stage, especially when such facts converge
with the results of the other approaches. (But note
the caveat in Fromkin.) The general convergence of
these approaches lends credence to the view that there
is a natural physiological and/or acoustical basis for
them all. But the air-stream features [nasal, voiced,
continuant, lateral] are scattered throughout the
hierarchy and two very assimilable features having
large neuromuscular indexes in Krmpotić's (1959) calculus of nerve sizes, [voiced] and [round], differ
vastly in their unmarked relative weightings in the
hierarchy. This does not mean, however, that a natural
basis for weighting will not be discovered. Chen MSb
found a natural basis for natural rule 6a in §3.1, and
the work of other scholars could be cited.

In the following hierarchical listing of the provisional unmarked relative weightings of features, a
list which has been generally found serviceable, only

fifteen of the twenty-three non-prosodic features, only
one of thirteen prosodic features, and only one of two
boundary features are included; [accent] and [word
boundary] are both non-phonetic (i.e. purely phonological) features[8],[6] while [peripheral] (Labov 1972a:161;
this feature has been included in the numbers cited
in the foregoing) may be a purely phonetic feature:

> 17. [nuclear]
> 16. [accent]
> 15. [word boundary]
> 14. [turbulent]
> 13. [nasal]
> 12. [liquid]
> 11. [voiced]
> 10. [continuant]
> 9. [sulcal]
> 8. [grave]
> 7. [lingual]
> 6. [vibrant]
> 5. [low]
> 4. [dorsal]
> 3. [pharyngeal widening]
> 2. [thyroid]
> 1. [round]

This list will doubtless undergo further revision and
expansion as the still incipient investigation of
weighting progresses. Further work is required to
determine whether flip-flops (like that of stark and
stork, card and cord, etc., in some Texas lects, which
exchanges m and u values of [round]) are amenable to
Principle 1 in any way. It is worth noting that the
two binary features to which any alleged ternary feature can be reduced entail different predictions about
feature-weighting from those implied by a single ternary feature; the two binary features imply a difference
in their relative weights which should be impossible in
the case of a single ternary feature. Note further that
the problem of marking the mid vowels in a binary-
feature system (cf. Chen MSa) is obviated in the ternary-
feature system.

   Two formalisms exist for building relative weights
into rules. Where the features are tautosegmental, the
heavier ones may simply be written (as suggested by
Bruce Fraser) above the lighter-weighted ones. Where

this notation is not possible, i.e. where the features do not belong to the same segment, numerical relative-weight operators may be employed, though without any claim that they are 'psychologically real'. What is psychologically real is the implicational arrangement which the relative heaviness and lightness of rule features generate according to Principles 9, 10, etc.

The calculus of feature weightings for a given rule environment is based on the numerical weight operators and the absolute (plus, mid, or minus) values, not the marking values, of their features[8][7] (Pending further investigation, the mid value of a feature is counted as zero and that feature then has no effect on the calculus.) In the calculus in Tables 1 and 2 in §3.1, two steps are seen. First, the absolute value of a variable feature is multiplied with the numerical operator. If the feature is negative and the operator is also negative, the result is positive. The sum of such values for all variable features then constitutes the weight of that environment.

NOTES

1. Views of the sort expressed in this writing are indicated in Bailey 1972 (summarizing a presentation given in early 1969) and in Bailey 1971.
2. Bailey 1972 advocated my present views on implicational patterning, the role of time in descriptive linguistics, and transpersonal language systems. Important theoretical work of the same period or earlier is to be found in Weinreich, Labov, & Herzog 1968 and in Labov 1972a (read at the same 1969 conference when Bailey 1972 was read)
3. The manifestations of parole are "individual and momentary" and are not homogeneous (Saussure 1962: 38 = 1959:19); language gets its unity from the social phenomenon of langue (1962:27 = 1959:11). References to Saussure are given for both the 1962 French printing of the third edition and the 1959 English translation; the renderings are my own throughout.
4. I am not unaware of rejections of the distinction between competence and performance by various linguists nor of new senses of the term performance being advocated by scholars in the social sciences who deal with language. Nevertheless, it does not seem possible for any scholar seriously to include in his analysis aspects of raw linguistic data which are unsystematic and unintended such as coughing, sighing, distortions due to eating, and the like. Slips of the tongue are another matter, and may be systematically predictable with an adequate marking theory; cf. fn. 36. I hope scholars who object to the distinction between competence and performance will be disarmed by my admitted aim of making the scope of performance as exiguous as possible, inoculating it from the harm it has brought to linguistic discussions in recent years through its use as

a waste basket for problems that linguists have
not wanted to face, preferring to treat them as
inessential or accidental. As for newer proposals by scholars in the social disciplines to
broaden the meaning of the term performance, the
reader will be excused from adopting either of
these because they run counter to his interest in
inoculating the term from the very serious confusions which it has already occasioned. (See
also fn. 36 below.)

5.   Bloomfield (1933:45) admitted "that no two per-
sons--or rather, perhaps, no one person at different times--[speaks] exactly alike".

6.   A later paradox of Hockett's is discussed in
Weinreich et al. 129.

7.   For a strongly dissentient view, see Foley 1970;
and cf. Shapiro 1972:345 fn. 6. Contrast the views
of the phonetician-phonologists Ohala (1971) and
Fromkin (1970). The writer's own advocacy of
naturalness below should not be construed as exclusively 'physicalist', any more than his favorable comments on the empirical aspects of linguistic study should be understood as a sign of hostil-
ity toward abstract entities in the mind, explanatory hypotheses, etc.; see §2.0. It is now widely
agreed that phonological changes, for example, may
be semantically and syntactically environed.

8.   As regards the final clause in the quotation from
Chomsky 1965 cited above, many scholars would be
of the opinion that a 'cogent reason' for modifying
the homogeneity doctrine had in fact been already
provided in Labov 1963.

9.   These differences are by no means necessarily of
equal probability in their occurrence in a speaker's
utterances. Not only linguists, but also language-
users themselves often tell us that certain usages
are frequent or usual, while others are not. Indeed, they may tell us that a given phenomenon depends on (implies) the presence of some other.
(Language-teachers tell students that when one calls
a man Monsieur, one addresses him with the pronoun
vous.)

10. Although it is styles that are spoken of in most of
the literature, I prefer tempo as the more objective
and quantifiable concept and one that corresponds

more intimately with the degree of monitoring of
one's own speech. As Bierwisch (1966) was able
to specify phrasings in terms of tempos, one can
also specify relative tempos in terms of phrasing
phenomena (cf. the simplification of Bierwisch's
approach and its adaptation to English in Bailey
MS).

11. Since I reject the term idiolect as the designation of any worthwhile notion, it is employed here
purely for expository purposes.

12. The formulation of interpersonal variants in a
single polylectal grammar representing language-
users' internalized competence is justified below
on the basis of the acquisition of language by
children.

13. "...the evidence has been disappointing: an un-
selected set of isoglosses does not divide a
territory into clear-cut areas, but rather into a
crosshatched continuum of finely subdivided fragments" (Weinreich et al. 151). In rejecting the
notion of dialect, Schuchardt (M-13) complained
against the notion of "a completely homogeneous
speech community" and against the practice of
"descend[ing] to the language of the individual
and specifically to its momentary average, in order
to find real homogeneity..." (Cf. fn. 11 above.)

14. Various coinages like sociolect and varilect, as
well as proposals to use idiom, variety, and tongue
for the purposes for which I am using lect have
their drawbacks. The first of these terms obscures
the similarity in principle between regional and
other social differences among varieties of a language. When dealing with creole continuums, it is
convenient to speak of the lect which is linguistically most remote from the prestige language as
the basilect; the prestige language of the area
may be called the matrilect or the acrolect. Further comments on the notion of dialects is found
in Bailey 1973b, where a number of implicational
patterns for English are cited and the possibility
of implicational patternings of lexical items is
discussed.

15. The similarities between Saussure's outlook and
that of E. Durkheim have led a number of scholars
to attribute to Saussure a greater influence from

Durkheim than was probably the case. In contrast
with Saussure's views, just quoted, to the effect
that past is past and present is present, Greenberg (1966:61) sensibly maintains that "some con-
nections between diachronic process and synchronic
regularities must exist, since no change can produce a synchronically unlawful state and all synchronic states are the outcome of diachronic processes."

16. Arthur Compton (personal communication) has ap-
prised me of some interesting aspects of a child's
non-instantaneous acquisition of English sounds.
At the stage when she was first investigated, the
child possessed three consonants in her repertoire:
[p m w]. One may assume the presence of the features [continuant] and [nasal] in her competence
at this point; [w] was used for adult [r] as well
as [w], so that ring sounded like wing. Then
[voiced] was acquired, adding [b] to her inventory
and [f] in opposition to [w]--which now got replaced with [v] as the voiced correlate of [f].
On the face of it, one might suppose that 'unlearn-
ing' the correct pronunciation of wing (now ving)
after it had been correctly pronounced would be
anything but optimal progress in the acquisition
of language. But in a framework of non-instantaneous acquisition of features, the child described here exhibited progress (in acquiring features) at every stage.

17. An exception to the reluctance of transformationalists to admit the effects of performance on competence is Bever & Langendoen 1972, beside Kiparsky
1972:222; see also Bolinger 1962. Kiparsky 1971
attributes instances of gradual sound change to
the allegedly scalar nature of phonetic features
(and would presumably now attribute semantic
changes to the fuzzy nature of semantic features).
The speciousness of this artifice becomes apparent
from the fact that the gradual raising of tense
/æ/ in New York City changes the plus-minus values
of two phonological features-- if they are binary.

18. A recent study maintaining the same general point
of view as the writer's is Householder 1972; cf.
also Bhat 1970. The primary document remains
Weinreich et al.

19. See Traugott 1973 for further discussion of the
     place of creolization in variation studies.
     Elsewhere I characterize natural changes result-
     ing from the manner in which children acquire
     their native languages as [+ natural]; changes
     due to borrowing from other systems are [x
     natural], where x represents the mid value of the
     feature; and [- natural] characterizes really un-
     natural developments (cf. fn. 29). Besides borrow-
     ing, other sources of increased markedness may be
     mentioned briefly. It is well-known that unmark-
     ing one segment may leave another marked. Since
     the markings are dependent on position within the
     syllable, according to the views of the present
     writer, epenthesis and deletion will greatly alter
     markings. See further fn. 24. Special markings
     also arise in order to distinguish different kinds
     of phenomena. Contrast the closed syllable in
     coyer and dualist with the open syllable (at least
     in 'r-less' lects) preceding an underlying sonoran-
     not preceded by a deleted underlying vowel in Maya
     lawyer, and hilly; and the rising diphthong in
     Fren. oui with the falling diphthong in bouille.
20. That recognition precedes production in child lan-
     guage has been recognized for a long while (e.g.
     Ervin 1964:164). It is too early to attempt
     answering such questions as whether rules begin
     variably in one's understanding competence before
     becoming (variable) rules in the subset of one's
     competence which is employed in producing speech.
     Because of the asymmetry between understanding and
     production (see §2.3), one might hypothesize that
     understanding is to be analyzed with binary fea-
     tures, while production is to be analyzed with
     ternary or scalar features. Such a difference is
     unlikely, and in any case listeners are able to
     scale what they hear, e.g. as more typical of a
     banker or telephone operator or as more typical of
     a ditch-digger.
21. Leveled varieties of a language exhibit the merger
     or neutralization of items which are unmerged in
     unleveled lects. The more items merged or not
     merged, the more leveled or unleveled the lect,
     respectively.
22. Since the orthodox transformationalists have

objected to polylectal grammars precisely on the
grounds of psychological reality, it is para-
doxical that many of them are now first to give
up the requirement of psychological reality in
their own work!

23. One of the most far-reaching investigations to
determine how well the ideas mentioned in this
paragraph stand up in the study of regional variation is being conducted by Gary J. Parker (cf.
MS), who has found that a number of problems which
were but artifacts of the old framework can now be
easily dealt with in the new.

24. Higher-level unmarkings can overrule feature unmarkings and result in the marking of previously
unmarked features. See Principal 1b in §3.0.
(Parker & Bailey 1970 suggest writing m upside-
down, i.e. as w, in such instances to show that
the new value is a natural one.) These higher-
level unmarkings include assimilation, dissimila-
tion, rule-reordering, chain shifts, crazy rules,
and perhaps others (e.g. flip-flops? See also
Vennemann's [1972b:240] typological adjustment rules
for the principle of symmetry). See also the discussion following rule 21 in this book, where the
compromise of two opposite values may result in an
M (overmarked) value. Polarization can easily be
illustrated with Hawaiian. When k became a glottal
stop in this language, t changed to k to become
maximally different from the only other stop re-
maining--p. Since t is unmarked for place of articulation in the syllable-initial position (see
the Appendix), this change represents a change of
[u lingual, u grave] to [w lingual, w grave].
Alternating accents represent a polarization of
maximal oppositions. The relation between marking
and chain shifts will be taken up again below; such
phenomena include the changes formalized with the
implicational (⊃ and ⊂) coefficients discussed below. Metathesis, epenthesis, and deletion often
change marked feature values to unmarked ones, and
may change the syllabication, accentual, and ryth-
mic patterns of a language. Note that unmarking
one feature may leave another marked. Intimately
connected with marking, but little understood (see,
however, Schane 1972:211, where the changes in

question fall under the rubric of polarization),
is what the writer calls <u>feature-stripping</u>. This
process deletes oral articulations for voiceless
or heavy stops (leaving them as [ʔ]), fricatives
(leaving them [h] or, if they were voiced, [ɦ]).
Similar to these is the change of liquids to the
voiced glides [y w], depending on their place of
articulation.

There is a problem with chain shifts, which
appear to be almost the only way that certain
fricatives--[ɸ þ ð], if not [ƀ], arise. (Similarly, [ç] is generated only in higher-level un-
markings--assimilation, in this case.) Given that
such changes begin gradually, in accord with Principle 2, one must ask how a language-user knows
that a given change is but the first step in a
shift, rather than a single change, say of //b// to
[ƀ]. Do changes begin one way, and then get converted to another species? Or are all such changes
potentially chain changes, always affecting certain
classes of fricatives before others? Much empirical evidence is yet needed to answer such questions.

Another aspect of these questions is that languages seem to group into two classes of related
prosodic phenomena. The A class has either no accent
or one which does not combine pitch and length;
syllable-timed rhythm; little vowel-weakening; unmarked syllabication (open syllables); rising
diphthongs (falling diphthongs would close syllables); liaison; full voicing of light consonants
next to boundaries and consonantal lenition; and
voice assimilation of an obstruent to a following
obstruent. There is a basic distinction between
open and closed syllables, if the latter exist in
type A languages. In type B languages, one finds
a heavy accent usually combining pitch and length
(so-called 'stress'); accent-timed rhythm; vowel-
weakening, syllabic sonorants, and syncope; marked
syllabication, with consonants clustering around
accented nuclei; falling diphthongs; apocope; devoicing of light obstruents next to boundaries and
consonant strengthening (as the High German consonant shift). Here there is a basic distinction
between open and loosely closed syllables (the
latter heard in <u>sane</u>, <u>deep</u>) vs. tightly closed

syllables (e.g. <u>sanity</u>, <u>depth</u>). See further on
accent in Jakobson 1968:33. Contrast the assimilation in French <u>opserver</u> and English <u>obzerver</u>,
<u>slipt</u>, <u>maps</u>. (<u>Lost</u> and <u>left</u> have a peculiar
history in that the penultimate obstruent in each
was the underlying one; it became an obstruent of
the light order in <u>lose</u> and <u>leave</u> between vowels.)
In type A languages ∥x∥ palatalizes before front
vowels and vowels often nasalize after nasal consonants; in type B languages, ∥x∥ palatalizes after
front vowels (e.g. German), and vowels often nasalize before nasal consonants.

   Note that 'r-less' English distinguishes
marked and unmarked syllabication of underlying
obstruents, the former syllabication (agreeing
with that of obstruents) being used for special
cases, viz. where a glide is generated from a
single underlying vowel or where a satellite liquid
results from a vowel-deletion (Bailey 1968a). In
French, where all consonants prefer unmarked syllabication in lento tempo, we find marked syllabication being used for special cases; contrast
normal [wi] in <u>oui</u> with [u^i] in <u>bouille</u> (where an
earlier lateral has been lost). Latin changed
from type A to type B in Romance, perhaps as the
result of many losses of unaccented vowels. Portuguese seems to be changing, for whatever cause,
back to a type A language, with vowel-weakening
and falling diphthongs (and few rising ones; cf.
Port. <u>fogo</u> with Span. <u>fuego</u> 'fire').

25. The writer's conventions for marking ternary (non-
prosodic and prosodic) phonetic features, which
markings depend on a segment's position in the
syllable and on the marking of heavier-weighted
features, are given in the Appendix. The definitions could be replaced with <u>natural rules</u> (see
§3.1; cf. the <u>natural processes</u> of Stampe 1969).

26. Although it has been fashionable in post-Saussurian
circles to think of sense and sound as the content
and expression of the grammar (somewhat reversing
the relation of form and matter in scholastic
thought), we may think of both semantics and phonetics as the matter of the grammar with respect
to content and of phonetics and morphonology as
the matter and form of the grammar with respect to
its expression.

27. Cf. also the seven points listed in Weinreich et al. 187-8.
28. It will become evident in §3 that rate in the present discussion is far from having any connection with the use of this term in glottochronology, between which and his own position the writer would admit no connection.
29. Dying languages exhibit the opposite directionality, as once-categorical rules become variable (Dressler 1972). This development is [- natural].
30. I am taking it for granted that mixtures of systems spoken by native speakers--i.e. creoles--may occur in different proportions and degrees, like the process of decreolization, which consists of recreolizing the basilect and the mesolects with the acrolect. Let scientists borrow pairwise from German (helped by English otherwise, which, however, is a de-adjectival adverb), and let -wise become a productive formative in ordinary speech for deriving adverbs from nouns, and this is creolization! But one would not wish to speak of creolization where only a few lexical items were borrowed--in fact, not until relexification reached massive proportions, the amount probably depending on the social situation-- because, as Bloomfield (1933:274) noted, the lexicon is a list of irregularities, of exceptional and other unpredictable aspects of a language. For new insights into the systematicity of the lexicon, see now Labov 1973.
31. For the different species of creolization and a brief discussion of decreolizing gradatums and other issues under consideration here, cf. Bailey 1973a. See also the end of §4.4.
32. Unmarked is abbreviated u: marked, m; and, in a ternary system, over-marked is M. My usual practice is to place lexical phonological representations inside double slants, representations for some point in a derivation between underlying lexical representations and phonetic outputs in single slants, and phonetic outputs themselves in square brackets. Names of features are also enclosed within square brackets.
33. Formalisms for indicating feature weighting in rules, together with comments on how relative

weightings are ascertained, are found in the
Appendix. See also on the coefficients ⊂ and ⊃
below. Kim 1966:82-83 has proposed the coefficient ⋓ for polar opposites; if ⋓ stands for
plus, then ⋓̄ (not ⋓̲) will stand for minus, and
conversely. A method of calculating environment
weightings is outlined in the Appendix and illustrated in the text later on.

34. All u̲ values are equally unweighted; there are no
differences resulting from different feature
weightings.

35. Specifying that the segments follow a nucleus is
necessary because of the different markings of
place and manner features of obstruents in the
special positions (immediately following a tautosyllabic accented vowel, where the marked value of
[nuclear] is minus; and preceding another obstruent in the prenuclear part of a syllable) and in
other environments. Thus, apical consonants are
more expected immediately before tautosyllabic
vowels than labials; and these are more expected
in this environment than velars. But in the special positions, except for fricatives, velar consonants are more expected than labials, and these
than apicals. See the Appendix. Since Rumanian
opt (from octō) cannot rightly be ascribed to
assimilation, as has been claimed, this change
constitutes something of a problem for the present
view of marking, although it is confirmed by a
vast number of changes, attested slips of the
tongue, etc.

36. When speech becomes extremely unmonitored as the
result of haste, fatigue, or emotional upsets,
marked phenomena progressively get replaced by the
corresponding unmarked phenomena. In terms of the
concepts proposed by Stampe (cf. fn. 25), who first
theorized on the matter, haste, fatigue, and emotional upset break down the monitored suppression
of natural rules, which are then permitted to
operate freely. Some natural rules are given at
the end of §3.1 in an implicational formalism.
Studies of different sorts have established that vic-
tims of the apraxia of speech may exhibit changes
which occur in a sequence which reverses the sequence of their acquisition by most children. And

Sasanuma & Fujimura 1971, building on older
studies, have carried on additional investigations to show that the functional losses of ideo-
grams and phonograms are not parallel in Japanese.
The systematicity of the 'disintegration' of
speech (e.g. in slips of the tongue) is sufficient
to indicate that even performance variables are
predictable and may some day be included in grammars. Undoubtedly some changes in languages begin
as slips of the tongue or unintended unmarkings in
unmonitored speech, just as others (over-corrections; see below) begin in over-monitoring. Predictions relating to such matters properly belong
to a theory of linguistic competence, in my opinion. Unmarking should soon account for the things
which Sapir (1921) discussed under the rubric of
'drift', as well as the so-called 'conspiracies'
of more recent vintage.

37.   There is, of course, nothing 'unnatural' or unusual in such borrowings. As already noted,
borrowings have the mid value of the feature
[natural]!

38.   The directionality of change from marked to unmarked may be set aside in borrowing between language systems--creolization--as already observed.
Also, as the basilect or mesolects decreolize
through borrowing from the matrilect, items that
were unmarked in the lower-status lects may get
marked, reversing the directionality of natural
change.

The reconstructive task may present a special
type of problem, which can be illustrated by the
problem of deciding whether the word-final nasal
in PIE was *m or *n. This is a problem because the
markedness of the different nasals is different in
most environments from what is found in the special
position following tautosyllabic accented vowels
(it is quite comparable to the same special position for obstruents; cf. fn. 35). Contrast the
usual changes of //m// to /n/ to [ŋ] in the word-final
environment (Chen MSb: diagram 1) with the change
of //ŋ// to [n] in allegro tempos after unaccented
vowels in English. Where a language permits a
neutralized word-final nasal after accented and unaccented vowels alike, as PIE does, either nasal

could--so far as is now known--be generalized to
the other by a 'crazy rule' of the sort discussed
in Bach & Harms 1972. It is premature to try to
guess whether the directionality of such generalizing processes will be predictable under constraints yet to be discovered.

39. Principle 2b may well be connected with the general
application priority of 'properly inclusive' formulations over those included by them according to
the principle first proposed by Gerald A. Sanders
(according to Koutsoudas, Sanders, & Noll 1971:10).
This general principle accords well with the principle governing the application of disjunctive
notations in Chomsky & Halle 1968:30 (since discussed in Anderson 1969), as well as the so-called
A-over-A principle in syntax.

40. The feature is [w.b.]. See below on the effects
of the morpheme boundary in pas+t. To obviate a
confusion into which some glottometrists have
fallen, it may help to state that there is no pho-

netic clustering at the end of crank ['khrã^{i}k],
work ['w₃:k 'weⁱ:k 'w₃k], and board ['boᵉ:d
'boᵉd] ([o] is over-rounded in BVE and Deep Southern White speech; [b] is injective in BVE and
fortis in Deep Southern White pronunciation). Contrast the lateral cluster in old ['oᵘl(d)] and
build ['b+ᴸ:(d)] in BVE and Southern pronunciation.
In the rules that follow, # symbolizes an internal
and ## an external word boundary.

41. The feature [u nuclear] denotes vowels in this environment; [m nuc] indicates non-vowels, which
class includes boundaries as well as consonants.
A number of factors which are ignored in the rules
may be mentioned; since the rules are purely illustrative here, incorporating these complications
would not serve the purpose or be compensated by
any advantages. Investigators of both BVE and
Southern States White English have found that the
deletion of a clustered word-final apical stop is
more likely if it ends an unaccented syllable than
if it ends an accented syllable; e.g. breakfas(t),
fores(t), den(t)is(t), fastes(t), ribal(d), husban(d),
and diamon(d). (The first ǁtǁ in dentist is deleted by another rule irrelevant to this discussion,

but discussed below in connection with <u>sentence</u>.)
My own researches of English in the Southern
States indicate not only that the deletion of //t//
clustered with a preceding obstruent and of //d//
clustered with a preceding //n// or lateral is least
likely before //h// or a vowel; but also that the
deletion is normal only before an obstruent (e.g.
<u>wastepaper</u>, <u>restful</u>, <u>left goal</u>, <u>handbag</u>, <u>windmill</u>,
<u>oldster</u>; cf. <u>acts</u>, <u>opts</u>, <u>rafts</u>, etc.) or a nasal
or lateral (e.g. <u>goldmine</u>, <u>landlocked</u>, <u>shiftless</u>,
<u>exactly</u>, <u>softly</u>, <u>least likely</u>, <u>first news</u>, <u>worst</u>
<u>mess</u>). (But epenthesis may restore a lost //d// in
<u>handler</u>.) Before /y/, the deletion of an apical
stop depends on whether the palatalization rule
follows (e.g. <u>jus' yet</u>, <u>las' year</u>) or precedes
rule 3; in the latter case, we have [st$^{\check{s}}$] or [$\check{s}$t$^{\check{s}}$]
in <u>just yet</u> and <u>last year</u>, as well as in <u>question</u>,
<u>bestial</u>, etc. Note that //t// is always palatalized
in the last examples, as well as in <u>vesture</u>, etc.
Before //r// and //w//, the deletion of a clustered
apical stop depends on the syllabication, which
differs for the two sonorants when they are followed by an unaccented vowel. Compare the retention of syllable-initial //t d// before //r// in
<u>vestry</u> (contrast <u>ves'ment</u>), <u>laundry</u>, and <u>foundry</u>
with their variable deletion (more likely in more
rapid tempos) when syllable-final before //w//, as
in <u>westward</u> and <u>landward</u>. Before //r w// plus accented vowels, there are two possible syllabica-
tions of clustered apical stops; cf. <u>once tried</u>,
<u>run dry</u>, <u>twice twenty</u>, <u>tool drawer</u> with <u>jus(t)</u>
<u>right</u>, <u>lan(d) rights</u>, <u>mus(t) win</u>, <u>trus(t)worthy</u>,
and <u>gol(d) rush</u>.

    Note that in normal tempos the difference be-
tween the presence of [t] in the phonological type
exemplified in <u>piston</u> and <u>pistol</u> and the absence
of [t] in the type exemplified by <u>mois(t)en</u> and
<u>nes(t)le</u> (where no underlying vowel follows //t//)
may be eliminated through a reordering which causes
the deletion of //t// in <u>restin'</u> and--if the speaker
is 'r-less'--in <u>western</u>. For further complications
of this rule, see Bailey 1973c.

42. Note that the heaviest and lightest environments
are the same in both 4a and 4b, while the middle
environments are reversed (cf. Labov 1972a:124).

Table 1 is brought into accord with Principle 8b
(§3.2) in Table 4 below (§4.1).

43. Some of the writers just cited have also arrived
     at the position, first advocated in Stampe 1969,
     that unmarked ordering is equivalent to non-
     ordering. The point will be amplified later
     (§3.1).
           Since this writing was submitted to the
     publisher, a conference on rule ordering has taken
     place at the University of Indiana (April, 1973).
     The publication of papers from that conference
     will be of supreme interest to readers interested
     in rule ordering.

44. In addition to the examples of different rule
     orderings that either differentiate lects of
     English or mark off lexical exceptions from other
     lexical items in the same lect which are given
     below, cf. Bailey MSb, where thirty or forty such
     differences are listed.

45. The change does not occur in American 'r-less'
     lects before the geminate /r/ which is automati-
     cally generated in American and British English
     between /ɚ/ and a following vowel, as in covering,
     Southern States ['khʌvɚrɪn]. See Bailey MSc for
     details of this process, which also affects the
     other sonorants.

46. In the Southern States, a lateral which is non-
     nuclear at the stage of derivation where rule v
     applies is not affected by the rule when it fol-
     lows a heavy (tense) rounded back nucleus; e.g.
     tool ['thʉᵘl], mule ['müᵘl], gule ['giᵘ̈l], goal
     ['goᵘl], ball ['bɔl 'bɒᵒl], and howl ['hæᵒl]
     (contrast Northern ['thuɫ:], etc., where rule v
     has applied). But a syllabic lateral, generated
     out of unaccented /əl/, is affected by rule v even
     in such environments; e.g. dualist ['dyuɫlɪst] and
     dual ['dyuɫ:], from /'diᵘɫ/ from /'diü̈ɫ/ from
     /'diᵘəl/ from ∥dual∥, as in duality. In like
     fashion are generated fluid ['flʉʹd] and poet
     ['phoʹt] from /'fluɪd/ (cf. fluidity) and /'poɪt/
     (cf. poetic). Not only is rule v more general
     than formulation v in these respects: it also
     applies to ∥r∥, as in pore ['phoᶿ:] and Jer'
     ['dž̆ɛᶿ:], with [ᶿ:] from [ɚ] by the late desul-
     calization rule; contrast 'r-less' Southern

porous ['phoᵘrəs] and <u>Jerry</u> ['dᶻɛrɪ], where
rule v has not applied, with the 'r-ful' pronunciations ['phoᶿrəs] and ['dᶻɛᶿri], where the
gemination of //r// before a vowel has created an
environment in which rule v (in its more general
formulation affecting //r// as well as //l//) can
operate. Compare the parallel gemination of //l//
and the operation of rule v in <u>dualist</u> above and
in Northern <u>silly</u> ['s₊ˡli] (contrast Southern
['sɪlɪ]). (The length mark is omitted between
such geminates.) An example with //r// that parallels <u>dual</u> above is <u>mower</u> ['moᶿ 'moᶿ:] from
/'moᵍ/ from /'moər/.

47. A later Southern States rule deletes /l/ in all
but lento tempos in the environment, V́ __ y V̆,
where V̆ is an unaccented vowel. The change of
heavy //ā// (cf. <u>prevail</u>) to /ă/ in <u>value</u> is due
to trisyllabic lightening; in <u>valiant</u>, it makes
sense only if the strong cluster /ly/ is created
before the application of the rule that lightens
nuclei in this environment, since normally a non-
high vowel becomes heavy before unaccented /ĭ/
followed by a vowel.

48. For <u>valiant</u> and <u>million</u> the illustration here requires replacing rule vi with a rule that changes
unaccented syllabic sonorants (including high
vowels) to their corresponding non-nuclear phones
before unaccented vowels. Thus, in the unmarked
ordering, the substitute rule vi would change
/'valiənt 'miliən/ to /'valyənt 'milyən/, and
rule v would convert this into /'vaˡ:yənt
'miˡ:yən/, which later rules would change to the
phonetic output of Northern States English:
['væˡ:yẽt 'm₊ˡ:yən]. Contrast Southern States
['væ(l)yẽt 'mɪ(l)yən]. Note that even a word
boundary does not count as a non-vowel: Southern
States <u>tell#it</u> ['thɛlɪt], <u>hill#y</u> ['hɪlɪ]. The
justification for the # in <u>hilly</u> is given in
Bailey MS; note that a phonological-phrase boundary does cause rule v to operate in the South as
well as elsewhere. Note the operation of the late
rule described in fn. 47 across the word boundary
in <u>will you</u> ['wɪyə -yə].

49. It may not be amiss to observe that a good theory

is a good discovery procedure. In addition to
examples later in this article, the following may
be instanced. Standard and non-standard pronunciation in the Southern States change //z// to /d/ in
isn't, doesn't, hasn't, and wasn't. Non-standard
pronunciation also has a rule, absent in standard
pronunciation, that changes /d/ to /t/ in the same
environment (as in couldn't and shouldn't), which
is converted finally to a glottal stop by a rule
which is found in most parts of the United States.
Since non-standard Southern States English has the
two main rules in their unmarked order, so that
//z// → /d/ → /t/, the analyst is naturally led to
seek relics of an earlier situation in which the
rules had their marked mutual ordering. This
would be a lect with ['ɪdn̩t] for isn't and ['š+ʔn̩t]
for shouldn't. Note also that holes in implicationally ordered natural developments lead the
linguist to seek the representative lects, either
to corroborate or to discorroborate some aspect of
his theory of language.

50. Creole studies are confirming the independence of
the components. The independence of the lexicon
has long been recognized; cf. now Gumperz & Wilson
1971. Carol Odo (MS) has found that young Hawaiian children may pronounce the velar nasal in the
formative -ing, a phonological trait of formal
style, while at the same time deleting the copula,
a syntactic characteristic of informal speech.
Cf. also Sasanuma & Fujimura (see fn. 36).

51. It is also probable that all adult-acquired linguistic phenomena are marked. If true, this would
mean that adults would have as much trouble learning the apical trill as the more marked uvular
trill, which in Europe has been borrowed to replace
the apical one.

52. Cf. Sapir 1921:174: "We may venture to surmise that
while whom will ultimately disappear from English
speech, locutions of the type Whom did you see?
will be obsolete when phrases like The man whom I
referred to are still in lingering use". (I am
indebted to William Peet for this citation.) The
Grecist will be familiar with the facts in Lejeune
1955:148-56, showing that in Ancient Greek *w was
progressively deleted in an implicationally pat-

terned succession of environments. These can be
generated with variable rules.

53. Charles Ferguson (personal communication) has
found in Ethiopia three results of a change in
the usual position of the verb from its older
location. Neighboring languages exhibit the
following temporally successive situations:
(a) the expected relation between verb position
and pre/postpositions has been obliterated;
(b) an interim alternation between prepositions
and postpositions has resulted; (c) a readjustment of the particle position has resulted in the
expected implication.

54. Elsewhere I have employed the coefficients [↑]
and [↓] for gradient (ternary-valued) features in
intonational analysis (cf. Bailey MS). The first
use of such arrows was by Fred Householder (personal communication) in another connection.

55. Contrast my Principle 1b with the way Schachter
employs the natural value; and note that the assi-
milated [+ nasal] is [m nasal] in the vowel, but
[u nasal] in the consonant in the special position

56. Principle 9a is evidently counterintuitive, since
a lighter-weighted feature, or one with the least
effects on a rule's operation, is obviously very
close to being generalized--i.e. irrelevant to the
rule. The writer began with this assumption, but
the variable segment in the environment of rule 11
below shows why 9a has been proposed. Here a
generalized [nasal] includes [u nasal], the last
environment to become operative and the slowest of
the three operative environments (before reweighting occurs). Hence, the feature specifying the
slowest environment, the lightest, must be the
last feature in the variable segment of the environment to be generalized. No doubt further
investigation will show a way to make Principle 9a
generalize lighter-weighted features before heavier
ones.

There is a psychological problem, related to
one discussed in fn. 24. This is the question of
how a language-user knows that [nasal] is a variant in rule 11 so long as it has only its marked
value and the nasal environment has not become
effective in the rule. Unless the language-user

already knows that [nasal] is the lightest feature on the basis of its relative weighting in
other rules of the lect, it does not seem possible
that he or she would know this until [nasal]
generalized and the nasal environment came into
play; but one will, of course, then know that it
is the lightest-weighted feature in the environment segment.

57.   It is a matter that awaits future investigation to
determine which instance of a feature environing
either side of an input is the one to be affected
by Principle 9. It seems unlikely that the same
feature could have different weightings in one
part of a given rule, but until the relevant
examples have been investigated in detail, this
matter has to be left up in the air.

58.   Features are heavier or lighter, but environments
are not only heavier and lighter, but faster and
slower according to their relative heaviness.
Since environment weightings depend not only on
feature weightings but also on their values (see
fn. 87), a heavier feature may be faster or slower
than a lighter one according to its plus, mid, or
minus values. In order for heavier-weighted variable features to have greater effects on the rate,
it is necessary, as explained in §3.3, for lighter
variable features to change (reverse) their values
oftener than heavier ones. This seems to contradict Principle 10a, but it should become clear below that it does not; see Principle 13 in §3.3.
A more formal statement of Principle 10 (using $\underline{F}$
for $\underline{feature}$, $\underline{W}$ for $\underline{weight}$, $\underline{R}$ for $\underline{rate}$, and parentheses for variability) is: (a) Where $W_{(F_j)} >$
$W_{(F_i)}$, then: $R_{(F_j)} > R_{(F_i)}$; (b) where $[\alpha\ F_i]$, then:
$R_{m,M} > R_u$; and (c) where $[\supset F_i]$, $R_+ > R_x > R_-$, and
where $[\subset F_i]$, $R_- > R_x > R_+$. (Cf. also Principle 19
in §4.1.)

59.   The reader is cautioned that a quite different
analysis is found in Labov 1972a. Using a kind of
vowel-space continuum, as it does, it may be more
in accord with the new framework than the present
analysis. But acoustical research (e.g. Stevens
1968) over the past years has convinced the writer

that there are optimal articulatory points
having quantal acoustic results which dominate
the phonologies of particular languages in that
the ideal places of articulations for their
sounds tend to converge at such points. (Cf.
also Fromkin 38-39 and fnn. 17 and 81.) To assert
that a speech sound has an idealized articulatory
focus or target is not to deny that such sounds
are actualized as a compromise between such ideal
targets and the targets of adjacent sounds, in
accordance with a temporal factor and a coefficient
for the degree to which the target of the sound
being articulated can be affected by other sounds.
Note that the phonetic rules in Öhman 1967 include
a temporal factor! All of this is quite another
matter from asserting that there are phonological
features which are non-scalar and there are phonetic features which are scalar, since (if the
present position is correct) there are as many
phonetic targets for a feature as there are phonological values of it.

60. The marking of [pharyngeal widening] or 'tense-
ness' in vowels is not without its problems. While
it is true that languages lacking the distinction
between 'tense' and 'lax' accented vowels normally
have only the former, it is also indubitably true
that 'tense' vowels are preferred in open accented
syllables, while 'lax' ones are more expected in
closed accented syllables. But this last may be
some sort of assimilatory phenomenon. Since rule
11 tenses /æ/ mainly in closed syllables, it appears to contravene Principle 1a. Note that this
change rarely affects paroxytonic syllables, which,
however, are in English also closed if an obstruent
follows the accented vowel.

61. The rule would progress quite well through three
environments if the environment were specified as
[⊃ continuant], but this would not happen in the
right sequence. Even if this were not a problem,
changes in the rate of the three environments and
the acceleration which is described below could not
be generated without the features in rule 11 and
the principles of generalization and reweighting
proposed here.

62. The situation is quite different with Greek-letter

variable coefficients, since a generalization of
the unmarked value to the marked as well as unmarked values causes an acceleration of the marked
values ahead of the unmarked one, in accordance
with Principle 10b.

63. Besides monosystematic speech communities, there
are two kinds of polysystematic speech communities.
One has closely related overlapping systems in use.
This is the decreolizing gradatum. Another polysystematic speech community has several unrelated
or distantly related language systems in use. If
this situation persists for long, a kind of creole
would be expected to develop (cf. Gumperz and
Wilson 1971).

64. 'R-lessness' refers to the presence of rule iv
above; 'r-ful' speakers have the sulcal peak and
satellite [ɝ ɚ] in barter, mere, mirror, etc.

65. Psycholinguists ought to be able to tell us
whether it is easier for Irish speakers, who
alternate [e] and [ɛ] in mean : meant to understand lects in which the alternation here is between [i] and [ɛ] than conversely.

66. One would like to know whether users of English
who have a four-way distinction between informal
'Suzie', less informal 'Susan', more formal 'Miss
Susan', and most formal 'Mrs. Jones' are able to
deal more competently with the three-way distinction lacking 'Miss Susan' than conversely.

67. It is probable today that most adult varieties of
BVE are in the last stage of decreolization; i.e.
the BVE system has only a minimal difference from
the system found among cultured Blacks and Whites
and uncultured Whites.

68. Lects in which [ɚ] is heard after the nuclear peak
in carm, palm, and walnut have a different explanation which in fact also supports the view of an
internalized polylectal grammar. These lects belong to 'r-ful' speakers who have had a great deal
of contact with 'r-less' speech--or whose progeni-
tors have had this contact. From the phonetic outputs ['khɑːm 'khɒːm 'phɑːm 'phɒːm 'wɔːnət],
the language-users in question have inferred underlying //parm karm wɒrnut// on the basis of pairs
like card ['khɑːd 'khɒːd] and ['khɑɚd 'khɒɚd] in
their (understanding) competence.

69. Principle 14 implies a cerebral organization of
    variation in terms of sets within sets--Venn dia-
    grams. Any such storage principle in the brain
    would severely constrain the kinds of variation
    tolerated in languages. Note that it has been
    found that variant signs used by the deaf form an
    implicational series (Woodward MS).
70. The causes may be linguistic (cf. Wang 1969:135)
    or social.
71. Fig. 5 is a spatial presentation. If Fig. 5a were
    a Venn diagram (cf. fn. 69), the opposite impli-
    cation would obtain: $\underline{A} \supset \underline{B} \supset \underline{C}$.
72. In order to avoid the confusion that is current on
    both sides of the fence dividing sociologists from
    linguists, it should be stressed that, whatever
    problems deviant cases like the famous Nathan B.
    (Labov 1966:249-53) present for the sociolinguist
    or sociologist, such cases present no problems for
    the linguist, provided the subgrammars of such
    deviant language-users are among the subgrammars
    (perhaps they are the subgrammars used by other
    sociological groupings) generated within the over-
    all grammar of the language.
73. One expects the light order of vowels in closed
    syllables; hence the heavy order is marked in the
    input of rule 21. There is, however, evidence
    that [pharyngeal width] (note its use in rule 11
    for 'tenseness') is not the most appropriate fea-
    ture for the distinction between heavy and light
    nuclei. The 'laxing' or 'lightening' of the heavy
    vowels (cf. deep, serene) in depth and serenity is
    due to rhythmic shortening (see feature 36 in the
    Appendix). In depth, the lengthened cluster that
    follows shortens the nucleus; in serenity, the
    demands of accent-timed rhythm shorten accented
    nuclei as one or more unaccented syllables follow.
    This rhythmic shortening is gradient and acceler-
    ates the operation of rule 21, since later outputs
    are heard in Friday and writing than in died, flies
    and night. But the non-gradient, or decremental,
    shortening of nuclei that results from being fol-
    lowed by tautosyllabic heavy obstruents (see fea-
    ture 25 in the Appendix) retards the operation of
    rule 21; so later outputs are heard in bribe and
    ride than in ripe and write. Kolb's data reveal

another aspect of gradient shortening (input
[⊏ rhythmic length]) in that /ī/ has later outputs
in right-handed and wheelwright than in night (see
fn. 74 for fight). Later outputs are heard in
-wright, whose mid-accented status makes it shorter
than a fully accented syllable, than in right-,
which is shorter because of the following not fully
accented syllable. For the effects of shortening
on the Martha's Vineyard equivalent of rule 21, see
Labov 1972:123. For the Southern States, see fn. 76.

74.   A comparison of Table 8 with Fig. 10 will show that
      the change spread from the South northward. Where
      [a] is present for a given word in the southern
      part of the six northern counties, [i] in that word
      has already been pushed out of the North of England.
      The words employed in this study are not entirely
      consistent with other words of the same general
      type. In contrast with sky (where we find mostly
      [aᵉ]), eye has more [i] pronunciations than [aᵉ],
      and most of the [aᵉ] pronunciations are North of
      the [i] ones. It is not impossible that the old
      velar in eye slowed down the change there. But
      when we compare night (mostly [i]) with fight
      (almost all [εⁱ]), this explanation hardly holds
      up, and we must suspect whether the preceding
      labial in fight hastens the nuclear change. There
      is a known problem with velar environments, dis-
      cussed below, since the fastest environments for
      the rule are the velar and prevelar satellites,
      while the slowest environment for obstruents is
      the velar one. It is unlikely that reweighting
      would affect single lexical items. For right-,
      see fn. 73.

75.   In connection with this, it should be pointed out
      that Lehiste 1970:20 shows that, other things be-
      ing equal, vowels are universally shorter before
      labials than before apicals and velars. This means
      that what looks like incremental shortening has the
      accelerating effects of gradient rhythmic shorten-
      ing in rule 21, where labial environments are the
      fastest. As for the accelerating effects of gra-
      dient rhythmic shortening in paroxytones, other
      examples are known. DeCamp 1959:60 found that in
      San Francisco there are speakers who pronounce
      naughty like knotty while still preserving the

distinction of <u>caught</u> and <u>cot</u>. The writer has
also observed a speaker from Washington, D.C.,
who has [ɑ] in <u>foggy</u> but [ɔ] in <u>fog</u>.

76. The effects of rhythmic shortening are discernible in the Southern States only in clitics
(<u>our</u> is more likely to be [,aᵉ:] than <u>hour</u> is)
and in modifiers preceding their heads in rising
tunes. Compare [aᵉ] (Charlestonian [əⁱ]) in
<u>united</u> (where //t// has become [d]) and <u>ninety</u>
(where //t// is deleted) with [a] (Charlestonian
[ɑᵉ]) in <u>United States</u> and in <u>ninety-nine</u>. In
the last items rule 22 has the unmarked ordering
after the changes of //t// found in these words.
Note <u>typewriter</u>, where the first two syllables
both have [aᵉ] (Charlestonian [ɑᵉ]) in the des-
cending tune. (See further Joos 1942.)

Since <u>pint</u> (cf. <u>ninety</u> in fn. 75) has
[ãᵉ], not [ã] in cultivated pronunciation in
most of the Southern States, it is necessary to
assume either (1) that rule 22 follows the deletion of nasals when these are followed by
tautosyllabic heavy (underlying voiceless) obstruents, or (2) that rule 22 operates in the
environment of a following devoiced nasal in the
same way that it operates in the environment of a
following heavy obstruent.

It may be noted here that Charlestonian English has palatal [c ᴶ] before front vowels (including [a:] from //ar// as in <u>card</u>, but not before
[ɑᵉ] in <u>kite</u> and [ɑᵒ] in <u>cow</u>) and in <u>girl</u> (which
is fronted in British English and is heard by
some Japanese as <u>gyoru</u>). Substandard pronunciation has the palatals before [æᵒ] (which is standard elsewhere in the South) in <u>cow</u> and before all
instances of [ɝ]--not just <u>girl</u>, but also <u>curl</u>,
<u>gird</u>, etc. (Charlestonian is 'r-less' except for
[ɝ], a frequent situation.)

77. Fig. 11 is based in part on the data in Kurath &
McDavid 1961, but the writer has added necessary
supplements and emendations from his own observations. In Fig. 11 heavier-weighted outputs are
written beneath lighter-weighted ones.

78. Table 8 has not solved all the problems involved in
such portrayals. The suspicious absence of [a] for
<u>about</u> in lects -1, -3, and -5 may indicate that

they should have been placed to the left of 0, instead of to the right of it.

79. This was discovered and first discussed by Labov (1966).

80. Prenasalized stops like [^{m}b] are [- cnt] and [+ trb]; fricative nasals are [+ cnt, + trb]. All of these are [+ nas]. Fricative laterals and trills are [+ trb]. Some rules treat plain nasal consonants as [= cnt] segments, grouping them with continuants; other rules treat nasal consonants as [∓ cnt] segments, grouping them with stops.

81. If the trill-tap difference could ever be shown to involve reweighting, this would be evidence that the difference involves different features, since feature values presumably cannot reweight. A further complication is posed by the tentative inclusion of flaps as well as taps under the mid value of feature 15 above.

82. But [x trb] is highly marked here.

83. But when before [+ nas]: [+,u cnt] and [-,m cnt].

84. But [x trb] is highly marked here.

85. This expectation can be changed by polar oppositions, since languages with two kinds of wide-grooved sibilants normally have the convex-dorsum ([+ dor]) and concave-dorsum ([- dor]) opposites. Some varieties of Portuguese prefer postnuclear [š] to [s]; cf. Swiss German in both special positions.

86. The view that phonological and phonetic features differ by being fixed-valued and scalar, respectively, has introduced into linguistic discussions a number of confusions that could well have been avoided. Cf. further fnn. 17 and 59.

87. Larger numerical operators, whether negative or positive, have greater effects on the rate of a rule than smaller ones, whether negative or positive. But the effect of the positive or negative sign attached to such a numerical operator is seen in the actual calculus of the weight of a given environment.

BIBLIOGRAPHY

Agard, Frederick B. 1971. Language and dialect: some tentative postulates. Linguistics 65.7-25.

Anderson, Stephen A. 1969. West Scandinavian vowel systems and the ordering of phonological rules. Bloomington, Ind.: Indiana University Linguistics Circle.

Bach, Emmon and Robert T. Harms. 1972. How do languages get crazy rules? In: Stockwell and Macaulay, pp. 1-21.

Bailey, Charles-James N. 1968a. Dialectal differences in the syllabication of non-nasal sonorants in American English. General linguistics 8.79-91.

-----. 1968b. An untested idea on lexical exceptions to the regular ordering of the phonological rules of a language. ERIC/PEGS 25/2.

-----. 1970. A proposed qualification on Guy Carden's notion of a 'possible sub-dialect'. (Working papers in linguistics 2/8.) pp. 31-32. Honolulu: Department of Linguistics, University of Hawaii.

-----. 1971. Trying to talk in the new paradigm. Papers in linguistics 4.312-38.

-----. 1972. The integration of linguistic theory: internal reconstruction and the comparative method in descriptive analysis. In: Stockwell and Macaulay pp. 22-31.

-----. 1973a. Comment on papers presented at the firs plenary session. Twenty-third annual Georgetown Uni versity round table meeting: Sociolinguistics -- current trends and prospects, ed. by R.W. Shuy. (Monograph series on languages and linguistics 25.) pp. 89-98. Washington, D.C.: Georgetown University Press.

-----. 1973b. The patterning of language variation. Varieties of present-day English, ed. by R.W. Bailey and J. Robinson. New York: Macmillan (in press).

-----. 1973c. Variation resulting from different rule orderings in English phonology. In: Bailey and Shuy, pp. 211-52.

-----. MS. Southern States phonetics (Rev., to appear).

----- and Jean-Claude G. Milner. 1968. The major class features 'sonorant' and 'vocalic' and the problem of syllabicity in generative phonology: with a note on the feature 'high'. Washington, D.C.: ERIC/PEGS 19.

Bailey, Charles-James N. and Roger W. Shuy. 1973. New ways of analyzing variation in English. Washington, D.C.: Georgetown University Press.

Becker, Donald A. 1967. Generative phonology and dialect study: an investigation of three modern German dialects. Ann Arbor, Mich.: University Microfilms.

Bever, T.G. and D.T. Langendoen. 1972. The interaction of speech perception and grammatical structure in the evolution of language. In: Stockwell and Macaulay, pp. 32-95.

Bhat, D.N.S. 1970. A new hypothesis on language change. Indian linguistics 31.1-13.

Bickerton, Derek. 1971. Inherent variability and variable rules. Foundations of language 7.457-92.

-----. MSa. On the nature of a creole continuum. (To appear in Language.)

-----. MSb. Quantitative versus dynamic paradigms: the case of Montreal 'que'. In: Bailey and Shuy, pp. 23-43.

Bierwisch, Manfred. 1966. Regeln für die intonation deutscher Sätze. Studia grammatica 7.99-201.

Bloch, Bernard. 1948. A set of postulates for phonemic analysis. Language 24.3-46.

Bloomfield, Leonard.   1933.   Language.   New York:
    Henry Holt and Co.

-----.   1939 [1964].   Menomini morphophonemics.   Études
    phonologiques dédiées à la memoire de m. le prince
    N.S. Troubetzkoy (originally TCLP 8), pp. 105-15.
    University, Ala.: University of Alabama Press.

Bolinger, Dwight L.   1962.   Binomials and pitch accent.
    Lingua 11.34-44.

Browne, E. Wayles.   1972.   How to apply phonological
    rules.   (Q.P.R. 105, April 15, 1972.)   pp. 143-45.
    Cambridge: Research Laboratory of Electronics,
    Massachusetts Institute of Technology.

Butters, Ronald R.   1971.   On the notion 'rule of gram-
    mar' in dialectology.   CLS 7.307-15.

Cairns, Charles E.   1969.   Markedness, neutralization,
    and universal redundancy rules.   Language 45.863-85.

-----.   1970.   Some comments on the formulation of mor-
    pheme structure constrains in markedness theory.
    Papers in linguistics 2.59-82.

Carden, Guy.   1970.   Logical predicates and idiolectal
    variation in English.   (Report NSF-25.)   Cambridge,
    Mass.: The Aiken Computation Laboratory, Harvard
    University.

Chafe, Wallace L.   1970.   Meaning and the structure of
    language.   Chicago: University of Chicago Press.

Chen, Matthew.   MSa.   A note on binary features, sim-
    plicity metric, and marking conventions.

-----.   MSb.   Metarules and universal constraints in
    phonological theory.   (Read at the XIth International
    Congress of Linguists.)

-----.   MSc.   Predictive power in phonological descrip-
    tion.   (Read at First annual California linguistic
    conference, Berkeley, 1971.)

Chomsky, Noam.   1965.   Aspects of the theory of syntax.
    Cambridge, Mass.: M.I.T. Press.

----- and Morris Halle.   1968.   The sound pattern of
    English.   New York: Harper & Row.

DeCamp, David.   1959.   The pronunciation of English in
    San Francisco, Second Part.   Orbis.   8.54-77.

-----.   1971.   Toward a generative analysis of a post-
    creole speech continuum.   In: Hymes, pp. 349-70.

Dressler, Wolfgang.   1971.   Some constraints on phono-
    logical change.   CLS 7.340-49.

-----.   1972.   On the phonology of language death.
    CLS 8.448-57.

-----.   MS.   Vowel neutralization and vowel reduction.

Elliott, Dale, Stanley Legum and Sandra Annear Thompson.
    1969.   Syntactic variation as linguistic data.
    CLS 5.52-59.

Ervin [-Tripp], Susan M.   1964.   Imitation and struc-
    tural change in children's language   New directions
    in the study of language, ed. by E.H. Lenneberg,
    pp. 163-89.   Cambridge, Mass.: M.I.T. Press.

Fasold, Ralph W.   1970.   Two models of socially signifi-
    cant linguistic variation.   Language 46.551-63.

-----.   1973.   The concept of 'earlier-later': more or
    less correct.   In: Bailey and Shuy, pp. 183-97.

Fishman, Joshua A.   1971.   Sociolinguistics: a brief
    introduction.   Rowley, Mass.: Newbury House.

Foley, James.   1970.   Phonological distinctive features.
    Folia linguistica 4.87-92.

Friedrich, Paul.   1971.   Distinctive features and
    functional groups in Tarascan phonology.   Language
    47.849-65.

Fries, Charles C. and Kenneth L. Pike. 1949. Co-
    existent phonemic systems. Language 25.29-50.

Fromkin, Victoria. 1970. The concept of 'natural-
    ness' in a universal phonetic theory. Glossa
    4.29-45.

Gleason, Henry A. 1961. An introduction to descrip-
    tive linguistics. (Rev. ed.) New York: Holt,
    Rinehart and Winston.

Gordon, David and George Lakoff. 1971. Conversational
    postulates. CLS 7.63-84.

Grant, William. 1914. The pronunciation of English in
    Scotland. Cambridge: Cambridge University Press.

Greenberg, Joseph. 1966. Language universals. Cur-
    rent trends in linguistics:3, ed. by T.A. Sebeok
    et al., pp. 61-112. The Hague: Mouton and Co.

Greenberg, S. Robert. 1969. An experimental study of
    certain intonation contrasts in American English.
    (WPP 13.) Los Angeles: University of California.

Gumperz, John J. and Robert Wilson. 1971. Convergency
    and creolization: a case from the Indo-Aryan/Dravid-
    ian border in India. In: Hymes, pp. 151-67.

Hockett, Charles F. 1955. A manual of phonology.
    (Indiana University publications in anthropology and
    linguistics, memoire 11.)

Hoenigswald, Henry M. 1966. A proposal for the study
    of folk-linguistics. Sociolinguistics: proceedings
    of the U.C.L.A. sociolinguistics conference, 1965,
    ed. by W. Bright, pp. 16-26. The Hague: Mouton
    and Co.

-----. MS. Typology, reconstruction, and the I.-E.
    semivowels. (Read at the annual meeting of the
    Linguistic Society of America, San Francisco, 1969.)

Householder, Fred W. 1972. The principal step in lin-
    guistic change. Language sciences 20.1-5.

Houston, Susan. 1970. Competence and performance in
    child black English. Language sciences 12.9-14.

Hymes, Dell. 1962. The ethnography of speaking.
    Anthropology and human behavior, ed. by T. Gladwin
    and W.C. Sturtevant, pp. 15-53. Washington, D.C.:
    Anthropological Society of Washington.

-----. (ed.). 1971. Pidginization and creolization
    of languages: proceedings of a conference held at
    the University of the West Indies, Mona, Jamaica,
    April 1968. Cambridge: Cambridge University Press.

Jakobson, Roman. 1958. What can typological studies
    contribute to historical comparative linguistics?
    Proceedings of the eighth international congress of
    linguists, Oslo, 1957, pp. 17-25. Oslo: Oslo Uni-
    versity Press.

-----. 1968. Child language, aphasia, and phonological
    universals. (Janua linguarum Ser. min. 72.) The
    Hague: Mouton and Co.

Johnson, C. Douglas. 1970. Formal aspects of phono-
    logical description. (P.O.L.A. 2/11.) Berkeley,
    Calif. Phonology Laboratory, University of California

Jones, Daniel. 1964. An outline of English phonetics.
    (9th ed., reprinted with minor alterations.) Cam-
    bridge: W. Heffer & Sons.

Joos, Martin. 1942. A phonological dilemma in Canadian
    English. Language 18.141-44.

-----. (ed.). 1966. Readings in linguistics I. (4th
    ed.) Chicago: University of Chicago Press.

Karttunen, Lauri. 1968. What do referential indices
    refer to? Santa Monica, Calif.: The Rand Corporation.

Kazazis, Kostas. 1968. Sunday Greek. CLS 4.130-40.

Kim, Chin-Wu. 1966. The linguistic specification of
    speech. (WPP 5.) Los Angeles: University of Cali-
    fornia, Los Angeles.

-----. 1970. A theory of aspiration. Phonetica
   21.107-16.

King, Robert D. MS. Rule insertion.

Kiparsky, Paul. 1968. Linguistic universals and linguistic change. Universals in linguistic theory,
   ed. by E. Bach and R.T. Harms, pp. 170-202. New
   York: Holt, Rinehart and Winston.

-----. 1970. Historical linguistics. New horizons
   in linguistics, ed. by J. Lyons, pp. 302-15. London:
   Penguin Books.

-----. 1971. Historical linguistics. A survey of
   linguistic science, ed. by W.O. Dingwall, pp. 576-
   642. College, Park, Md.: Linguistics Program,
   University of Maryland.

-----. 1972. Explanation in phonology. Goals of linguistic theory, ed. by Stanley Peters, pp. 189-225.
   Englewood Cliffs, N.J.: Prentice-Hall.

-----. MS. How abstract is phonology? Bloomington,
   Ind.: Indiana University Linguistics Circle.

Klima, Edward S. 1964. Relatedness between grammatical systems. Language 40.1-20.

----- and Ursula Bellugi [-Klima]. 1966. Syntactic
   regularities in the speech of children. Psycho-
   linguistics papers: the proceedings of the 1966
   Edinburgh conference, ed. by J. Lyons and R.J. Wales,
   pp. 181-219. Edinburgh: Edinburgh University Press.

Kolb, Eduard. 1966. Phonological atlas of the northern
   region: the six northern counties, north Lincolnshire
   and the Isle of Man. (Linguistic atlas of England.)
   Bern: Francke Verlag.

Koutsoudas, Andreas. MSa. On the non-sufficiency of
   extrinsic order. Bloomington, Ind.: Indiana University Linguistics Circle.

-----. MSb. The strict order fallacy.

-----, Gerald Sanders and Craig Noll. MS. On the
    application of phonological rules. Bloomington,
    Ind.: Indiana University Linguistics Circle.

Krmpotić, Jelena. 1959. Données anatomiques et
    histologiques relatives aux effecteurs laryngo-
    pharyngo-buccaux. Revue de laryngologie, otologie,
    rhinologie 80.829-48.

Krohn, Robert. 1969. English vowels. Ann Arbor,
    Mich.: University Microfilms.

Kurath, Hans and Raven I. McDavid, Jr. 1961. The pro-
    nunciation of English in the Atlantic States: based
    upon the collections of the Linguistic atlas of the
    eastern United States. (Studies in American Eng-
    lish 3.) Ann Arbor, Mich.: University of Michigan
    Press.

Labov, William. 1963. The social motivation of a
    sound change. Word 19.273-309.

-----. 1966. The social stratification of English in
    New York City. (Urban language series 1.) Washing-
    ton, D.C.: Center for Applied Linguistics.

-----. 1969. Contraction, deletion, and inherent
    variability of the English copula. Language 45.715-62.

-----. 1972a. The internal evolution of linguistic
    rules. In: Stockwell and Macaulay, pp. 101-71.

-----. 1972b. Some principles of linguistic metho-
    dology. Language and society 1.97-120.

-----. 1973. Where do grammars stop? Twenty-third
    annual Georgetown University round table meeting:
    Sociolinguistics -- current trends and prospects,
    ed. by R.W. Shuy. (Monograph series on languages
    and linguistics 25.) pp. 43-88. Washington, D.C.:
    Georgetown University Press.

-----. MS. On the use of the present to explain the
    past. (To appear in the proceedings of the Eleventh
    international congress of linguists, Bologna, Italy,
    1972.)

Labov, William, Paul Cohen, Clarence Robins and John
    Lewis. 1968. A study of the non-standard English
    of Negro and Puerto Rican speakers in New York City,
    volume I: phonological and grammatical analysis.
    (Cooperative research project 3288.) New York:
    Columbia University.

Lakoff, Robin. 1972. Language in contact. Language
    48.907-27.

Lass, Roger. 1971. Sound shifts as strategies for
    feature-erasing: some evidence from Grimm's law.
    Bloomington, Ind.: Indiana University Linguistic
    Circle.

Lehiste, Ilse. 1970. Suprasegmentals. Cambridge,
    Mass.: M.I.T. Press.

Lehmann, Twila. 1972. Some arguments against ordered
    rules. Language 48.541-50.

Lejeune, Michel. 1955. Traité de phonétique grecque.
    (2d rev. & cor. ed.) Paris: Librairie C. Klinck-
    sieck.

LePage, Robert B. 1966. Foreword. Jamaican Creole
    syntax: a transformational approach, by Beryl Bailey.
    pp. v-viii. Cambridge: Cambridge University Press.

Loflin, Marvin D. 1971. On the structure of the verb
    in a dialect of American Negro English. Readings in
    American dialectology, ed. by H.B. Allen and G.N.
    Underwood, pp. 428-43. New York: Appleton-Century-
    Crofts.

McDavid, Raven I., Jr. 1940. Low-back vowels in the
    South Carolina Piedmont. American speech 15.144-48.

Miller, Patricia D. 1972. Some context-free processes
    affecting vowels. (Working papers in linguistics 11.
    pp. 136-67. Columbus, Ohio: Department of Linguis-
    tics, Ohio State University.

Morgan, Jerry. MS. Verb agreement as a rule of English

Morris, Charles. 1946. Signs, language and behavior. New York: Prentice-Hall.

Norman, Linda. 1972. The insufficiency of local ordering. CLS 8.490-503.

Odo, Carol. MS. English patterns in Hawaii. (To appear in American Speech.)

Öhman, Sven. 1967. Numerical model of coarticulation. Journal of the Acoustical Society of America 41.310-20.

Ohala, John J. 1971. The role of psyciological and acoustical models in explaining the direction of sound change. (P.O.L.A. 2/15.) pp. 25-40. Berkeley, Calif.: University of California, Phonology Laboratory.

Parker, Gary J. 1971. Comparative Quechua phonology and grammar V: The evolution of Quechua B. (Working papers in linguistics 3/3.) pp. 45-109. Honolulu: Department of Linguistics, University of Hawaii.

----- and Charles-James N. Bailey. 1970. Ternary markedness values: An approach to the measurement of complexity in the operation of phonological rules. (Working papers in linguistics 2/4.) pp. 131-42. Honolulu: Department of Linguistics, University of Hawaii.

Postal, Paul M. 1968. Aspects of phonological theory. New York: Harper and Row.

Ringen, Catherine. 1972. On arguments for rule re-ordering. Foundations of language 8.266-73.

-----. MS. Rule order and obligatory rules. (To appear in the proceedings of the Eleventh international congress of linguists, Bologna, Italy, 1972.)

Sankoff, Gillian. MS. A quantitative paradigm for the study of communicative competence.

Sapir, Edward. 1921. Language: An introduction to the study of speech. New York: Harcourt, Brace.

Sasanuma, Sumiko and Osamu Fujimura. 1971. Selective
    impairment of phonetic and non-phonetic trans-
    scription of words in Japanese aphasic patients:
    Kana vs. kanji in visual recognition and writing.
    Cortex 7.1-8.

Saussure, Ferdinand de. 1962 reprint. Cours de lin-
    guistique générale. (3d ed.) Paris: Payot.
    [1959, trans. by Wade Baskin as: Course in general
    linguistics. New York: Philosophical Library.]

Schachter, Paul. 1969. Natural assimilation rules in
    Akan. International journal of American linguistics
    35.342-55.

Schane, Sanford A. 1968. On the non-uniqueness of
    phonological representations. Language 44.709-16.

-----. 1972. Natural rules in phonology. In: Stock-
    well and Macaulay, pp. 199-229.

Schmidt, Johannes. 1872. Die Verwantschaftsverhältnisse
    der indogermanischen Sprachen. Weimar: Hermann
    Böhlau.

Schourup, Lawrence C. 1972. Why sound change is gradual
    (Working papers in linguistics 11.) pp. 127-35.
    Columbus, Ohio: Department of Linguistics, Ohio
    State University.

Schuchardt, Hugo. 1971. On phonetic laws against the
    neogrammarians, trans. by Burkhard Mohr. (P.O.L.A.
    2/12.) pp. M1-M33. Berkeley, Calif.: University of
    California, Phonology Laboratory.

Shapiro, Michael. 1972. Explorations into markedness.
    Language 343-64.

Stampe, David. 1969. The acquisition of phonetic
    representation. CLS 5.443-54.

-----. MS. How I spent my summer vacation. (University
    of Chicago Ph.D. dissertation.)

Stevens, Kenneth N. 1968. Acoustic correlates of place

of articulation for stop and fricative consonants.
(Q.P.R. 89.) pp. 199-205. Cambridge, Mass.:
Massachusetts Institute of Technology, Research
Laboratory of Electronics.

Stockwell, R.P. and Ronald K.S. Macaulay. 1972. Linguistic change and generative theory: Essays from
the UCLA conference on historical linguistics in
the perspective of transofrmational theory, February,
1969. Bloomington, Ind.: Indiana University Press.

Traugott, Elizabeth Closs. 1973. Historical linguistics and its relation to studies of language acquisition and of pidgins and creoles. In: Bailey and
Shuy, pp. 313-22.

Trudgill, Peter. MS. Geographical diffusion models
and explanation in sociolinguistic dialect geography.

Vennemann, Theo. 1972a. Phonological uniqueness in
natural generative grammar. Glossa 6.105-16.

-----. 1972b. Sound change and markedness theory:
On the history of the German consonant system.
In: Stockwell and Macaulay, pp. 230-74.

-----. MS. Rule inversion.

Wang, William S.-Y. 1969. Competing changes as a
cause of residue. Language 45.9-25.

Weinreich, Uriel, William Labov and Marvin I. Herzog.
1968. Empirical foundations for a theory of language change. Directions for historical linguistics,
ed. by W.P. Lehmann and Y. Malkiel, pp. 95-195.
Austin, Texas: University of Texas Press.

Woodward, James C., Jr. MS. Implicational lects on the
deaf diglossic continuum. (Georgetown University
Ph.D. dissertation.)

Wolfram, Walt. 1973. Sociolinguistic aspects of assimilation: Puerto Rican English in New York City. Washington, D.C.: Center for Applied Linguistics (in
press).

Zwicky, Arnold M.   1972.   Note on a phonological
    hierarchy in English.   In: Stockwell and Macaulay,
    pp. 275-301.